DK EYEWITNESS

T0063759

# TOP 10
# CRETE

# Top 10 Crete Highlights

# The Top 10 of Everything

# CONTENTS

## Crete
## Area by Area

## Streetsmart

Within each Top 10 list in this book, no hierarchy of quality or popularity is implied. All 10 are, in the editor's opinion, of roughly equal merit.

***Title page, front cover and spine*** *Picturesque harbour in the seaside village of Bali in Rethymno* ***Back cover, clockwise from top left*** *Windmills, Lasithi Plateau; the Venetian Harbour, Chania; a red-domed church on the cliff; Bali harbour; scenic street in old town, Rethymno*

The rate at which the world is changing is constantly keeping the DK Eyewitness team on our toes. While we've worked hard to ensure that this edition of Crete is accurate and up-to-date, we know that opening hours alter, standards shift, prices fluctuate, places close and new ones pop up in their stead. So, if you notice we've got something wrong or left something out, we want to hear about it. Please get in touch at **travelguides@dk.com**

# Welcome to
# Crete

Snowcapped mountains. Sandy beaches backed by palms. Turquoise-blue lagoons. Home of the ancient Minoans, a creative people who built their palaces here some 4,000 years ago. This is Crete, an extraordinary island that rises from the Mediterranean Sea south of mainland Greece. With DK Eyewitness Top 10 Crete, it's yours to explore.

The Minoans, who never developed an army since they had no enemies, are considered the world's first leisure civilization. So it seems appropriate that today, each summer, tens of thousands of holiday-makers flock to their island to bask in blissful sunshine and carefree escapism. Nowadays, visitors are attracted by Crete's golden sands and glistening waters, the informal seafood tavernas and hospitable locals, and the magnificent Venetian-era port cities of Heraklion, Chania and Rethymno.

Others come here to trace Crete's history and culture – to explore the timeless archaeological sites of **Ancient Knossos**, **Gortys**, **Phaistos** and **Spinalonga**, and to visit the fascinating **Archaeological Museum of Heraklion** and the melancholic **Moni Arkadi**. Adventurous outdoor enthusiasts are drawn to Crete's wild and dramatic unspoiled interior. They visit to hike the length of the **Samaria Gorge** or to cycle through the **Amari Valley** at the foot of **Mount Ida**. The foodies among them stop off at farm-shops, wineries and traditional tavernas to taste and buy wholesome local produce.

Whether you're visiting for a weekend or a week, our Top 10 guide brings together the best of everything that Crete can offer, from Ancient Knossos to the romantic harbour town of Chania. The guide has useful tips throughout – from seeking out what's free to avoiding the crowds – plus five easy-to-follow itineraries, designed to help you visit a clutch of sights in a short space of time. Add inspiring photography and detailed maps, and you have the essential pocket-sized travel companion. **Enjoy the book, and enjoy Crete**.

Clockwise from top: **Harbour at Loutro; windmills on the Lasithi Plateau; Moni Arkadi; the fortress of Frangokastello; murals at Knossos; the harbour at Chania; the lagoon at Balos**

# Exploring Crete

Crete is vast, stretching 260 km (162 miles) from east to west, and it really warrants at least one week, ideally two. Here are ideas for fitting the highlights – including ancient and modern sites, and indoor and outdoor activities – into a tight schedule. You'll need a car to keep up with these densely packed itineraries.

**This fresco fragment** is from Ancient Knossos.

**The Venetian fortress** at Rethymno sits on a rocky spur overlooking the sea.

**Key**
— Two-day itinerary
— Seven-day itinerary

## Two Days in Crete

### Day ❶
**MORNING**
Start at **Ancient Knossos** (see pp12–13), the ruins of a Minoan palace. Next, head to **Heraklion** (see pp16–17), Crete's capital, and explore the collection at the **Archaeological Museum of Heraklion** (see pp18–19).
**AFTERNOON**
Spend the afternoon in **Heraklion** (see pp16–17), with its car-free old town full of Venetian-era monuments. Later, drive to **Chania** (see pp20–21) and dine on seafood. Spend the night there.

### Day ❷
**MORNING**
Wander around **Chania** (see pp20–21), with its busy harbour and colourful market. Drive to **Rethymno** (see pp26–7) and arrive in time for lunch.
**AFTERNOON**
Explore Rethymno's Venetian fortress, then take time for a swim at the palm-lined beach east of the harbour. Return to **Heraklion** (see pp16–17) in the evening for dinner.

## Seven Days in Crete

### Day ❶
Devote your first day to **Chania** (see pp20–21), with its lovely old town. Visit the **Archaeological Museum** (see p49), then enjoy a swim at **Agioi Apostolii Beach** (see p21). Have dinner at **The Five Restaurant** (see p109) and drinks at **Synagogi Bar** (see p108).

### Day ❷
Devote today to a full-day excursion to the **Samaria Gorge** (see pp30–31). Wear good walking boots and carry a picnic lunch. This dramatic hike brings you down to the south coast at **Agia Roumeli** (see p65), with its pebbled beach. Have a swim, then take the coastal ferry to Chora Sfakion, where a bus will take you back to **Chania** (see pp20–21).

**The beach at Matala**, on Crete's southern coast, is sheltered by red cliffs.

### Day ❸
Drive along the coast to **Rethymno** *(see pp26–7)* and explore the old town's Venetian monuments. After lunch, go for a swim at Rethymno's palm-lined beach. Dine at **Avli** *(see p109)*, then go for cocktails at the **Garden of Ali Vafi** *(see p108)*.

### Day ❹
Explore Western Crete's interior. Drive to the fortified monastery of **Moni Arkadi** *(see pp36–7)*, with its 16th-century church and museum. Proceed to the remote **Amari Valley** *(see pp32–3)*, dotted with rural villages and Byzantine churches. Return to Rethymno for dinner.

### Day ❺
Drive westwards to **Ancient Knossos** *(see pp12–13)* to see the ruins of this splendid Minoan palace. Later, head to **Heraklion** *(see pp16–17)*, where you can explore the wonderful Venetian old town and see the treasures at the **Archaeological Museum of Heraklion** *(see pp18–19)*.

### Day ❻
Drive south across the island to two more archaeological sites: Roman **Gortys** *(see pp28–9)* and Minoan **Phaistos** *(see pp24–5)*. Take some time to explore the caves and white sand at **Matala** beach *(see p93)* before returning to **Heraklion** *(see pp16–17)*.

### Day ❼
On your final day, head east along the coast to **Gournia** *(see p42)*, another impressive Minoan site. Afterwards, have lunch in **Elounda** *(see p110)*. Take an afternoon boat trip from Elounda to the island fortress of **Spinalonga** *(see pp34–5)*, rising from the blue waters of the Gulf of Mirabello. Return to **Heraklion** *(see pp16–17)* for the evening.

# Top 10 Crete Highlights

The mosque within the ruined
Venetian fortress of Rethymno

# 📠 Crete Highlights

Although it belongs to Greece, Crete has its own clearly defined history and folklore. The Minoans flourished here over 4,000 years ago. Greeks, Romans, Byzantines, Saracens, Venetians and Ottomans also left their mark. This rich heritage is set against magnificent mountain scenery and beaches lapped by a deep-blue sea.

### Ancient Knossos ①

An impressive relic of the ancient Mediterranean world, the Minoan palace was imaginatively reconstructed in the early 1900s (see pp12–15).

### Heraklion ②

A good place to see a slice of everyday Greek life, Crete's capital is an eclectic mix of medieval Venetian fortifications, bustling markets and modern streets (see pp16–19).

### Chania ③

This pretty little harbour town, with good beaches nearby and plenty of open-air restaurants and shops, makes a great base for exploring Crete's wild west (see pp20–21).

### Phaistos ④

One of the main Minoan sites in Crete, Phaistos is a maze of courtyards and stairways on a hillside overlooking the Messara Plain and the Libyan Sea (see pp24–5).

Rodopou Peninsula
Akrotiri Peninsula
Kastelli
Platanias Chania ③
Souda Drepanon
Topolia
Nea Rumata
Georgioupoli
Rethymno ⑤ Panormos
Perama
Elos
Vati
Plemenian
Lefká Ori
Amudarion
Moni Arkadi ⑩
Paleochora
Samaria Gorge ⑦
Chora Sfakion
The Amari Valley and Mount Ida ⑧
0 km 25
0 miles 25
Agia Galini
Phaistos
Matala
Gavdos
Lithinos

### Rethymno **5**

Crete's third-largest city has had a multilayered history. A huge fortress, Ottoman mosques, Venetian townhouses and busy markets are part of the charm, along with a beach esplanade *(see pp26–7)*.

### **6** Gortys

Toppled Roman columns, the ruins of a Byzantine basilica, post-Minoan fortifications and remains of temples all hint at Gortys's chequered past *(see pp28–9)*.

### Samaria Gorge **7**

The "White Mountains" of the Sfakia region dominate southwest Crete. This rugged massif, most of which can be explored only on foot, is traversed by the lovely Samaria Gorge *(see pp30–31)*.

*Sea of Crete*

Heraklion **2**
Hersonissos
Malia
**9** Spinalonga
Ancient Knossos **1** Neapolis
Agios Nikolaos
Sitia
Vai
Sideros
*Aghios Ióannis*
*Oros Dikti*
Panagia
Agioi Deka
Marta
Gournia
Sikea
Kato Zakros
Pirgos
Ierapetra
Makrygialos
*Oros*
Gortys

### **8** The Amari Valley and Mount Ida

Old-fashioned villages and legend-laden caves can be explored with a car or on a guided coach tour *(see pp32–3)*.

### **9** Spinalonga

Fortified by a 16th-century Venetian fortress, this islet was one of the last active leper colonies in Europe *(see pp34–5)*.

### Moni Arkadi **10**

A place of tranquillity with a tragic past, the 16th-century Moni Arkadi is Crete's best-loved Greek Orthodox monastery *(see pp36–7)*.

# TOP 10 ⭐ Ancient Knossos

Knossos is steeped in mystery and enchantment. In legend, it was the seat of King Minos, beneath whose palace the bull-headed Minotaur hunted its victims in the labyrinth built by Daedalus. In reality, it was the hub of a Bronze Age empire that held sway over the Aegean more than 4,000 years ago. This part of the Knossos story began to be unearthed during the early 1900s, when British archaeologist Sir Arthur Evans began excavations of the site.

**1 Piano Nobile**
Dubbed the "noble hall" because it might have been the audience hall of the Minoan kings, this vast room features copies of the fabulous frescoes of leaping bull dancers – Knossos's most famous images.

**2 Storehouses**
The storehouses contain giant earthenware jars **(above)**, which the Minoans used to keep olive oil, olives, grain and other supplies. Such jars (*pithoi* in Greek), with a capacity of up to 200 litres, are still made today.

**3 Central Court**
All Minoan palaces were built around a central courtyard. This would have been the hub of the complex and likely been used for cere-monial purposes and for royal audiences. The courtyard of Knossos has a view of the valley.

**4 Throne Room**
Here, a stone throne stands next to a basin believed to have been used for ritual purification, perhaps before sacrifices were made to honour the gods.

**5 Dolphin Frescoes**
The queen's rooms were decorated with frescoes of leaping dolphins **(below)**, and equipped with a bath and even a flush lavatory.

**Ancient Knossos**

### 6 Hall of Double Axes

The hallway leading to the King's chamber is named after the double-bladed axe symbols carved into its walls and columns.

### 7 North Entrance Passage

A fresco of a bull adorns the entrance to this passage **(below)**. Images of sacred bulls outlasted the Minoan civilization and helped foster the legend of the Minotaur.

### 8 Great Staircase

Three smaller stairways and a maze of corridors would once have led off the five broad, shallow stone steps of the grand staircase **(below)**. Four of these wide steps survive to this day.

### 9 Bust of Sir Arthur Evans

A bust of Evans at the site entrance honours the man who first traced the palace of King Minos to this hillside above Heraklion. His sweeping reconstructions of the ancient palace owe much to his imagination.

### 10 South Portico

The south gateway to the palace complex **(left)** features copies of the Procession fresco, the original of which is in the Archaeological Museum of Heraklion *(see pp18–19)*.

**NEED TO KNOW**

**MAP K4** ■ Route 97, 8 km (5 miles) S of Heraklion ■ 2810 231940

**Open** summer: 8am–8pm daily (last adm 7:45pm); winter: 8am–3pm daily; closed or short hours on some national hols

Adm €18; concessions €10; combined ticket for Knossos and Archaeological Museum of Heraklion €20

■ If possible, visit Knossos in spring or autumn, when cooler weather makes exploring more pleasant than in high summer. However, if you are visiting in peak season, get to the site as soon as it opens, before most coach tour groups have arrived, or towards the end of the day.

■ There are several popular tavernas and decent snack bars within a few steps of the site entrance, along the main road to Heraklion.

# Archaeologists in Crete

Archaeological Museum of Heraklion, established by Joseph Hatzidakis

### 1 Joseph Hatzidakis

Crete's own Joseph Hatzidakis pioneered the search for relics of the island's distant past, winning permission from the Ottoman sultan to establish the Cretan Archaeological Society in the 1880s. The Society played a key role in locating and preserving Crete's major sites, and in setting up the Archaeological Museum of Heraklion *(see pp18–19)*.

Portrait of Heinrich Schliemann

### 2 Heinrich Schliemann

A famous archaeologist fascinated with the world of Homer's epics, Schliemann discovered first the site of ancient Troy (in Turkey), then Mycenae (in mainland Greece). In 1887, he turned his attention to sites in Crete, but he was unable to purchase the site of Knossos, leaving the field open for Sir Arthur Evans.

### 3 Sir Arthur Evans

Born into a wealthy British family, Sir Arthur Evans was educated at Oxford, where he later became keeper of the prestigious Ashmolean Museum. Crete's liberation from Ottoman rule in 1898, four years after his first visit to the site, made it possible for him to buy the site and begin work there in 1900. He devoted the next three decades of his life to Knossos.

### 4 Federico Halbherr

An Italian, Halbherr came to Crete in 1884 and befriended the Cretan archaeologist Joseph Hatzidakis, with whom he discovered the Bronze Age relics at the Dikteon Cave *(see p112)*. He later unearthed the palace sites at Phaistos *(see pp24–5)* and Agia Triada *(see p90)*.

### 5 John Pendlebury

One of the most colourful figures in Cretan archaeology, Pendlebury continued Evans' work at Knossos. He explored much of the island on foot and by donkey, pinpointing dozens of important sites. He also became a hero to Cretans after dying in action against the invading Germans in 1941.

### 6 Harriet Boyd-Hawes

This American archaeologist and nurse arrived on the island of Crete in 1900 and, after hunting for promising sites, surprised the archaeological world by unearthing a complete Minoan town at Gournia (see p42) between 1901 and 1904.

### 7 Richard Seager

Among the first American scholars to work in Crete, Richard Seager excavated the Minoan site at Vasiliki at the beginning of the 20th century, before starting work at Mochlos (see p114), where American archaeologists still work with Greek researchers today.

### 8 Alan Wace

The prominent director of the British School at Athens, Alan Wace clashed with the opinionated Arthur Evans when his discoveries at Mycenae on the mainland led him to claim (correctly) that the Mycenaean culture had not been an offshoot of the Minoan, but had existed independently and had eventually come to control Knossos.

### 9 Minos Kalokairinos

This Cretan businessman and amateur archaeologist first dug at Knossos in 1878, finding fragments of Mycenaean pottery and large storage jars, but was unable to buy the site. His discoveries brought Knossos to the attention of Heinrich Schliemann.

### 10 Nikolaos Platon

The instincts of this Greek archaeologist led to the rediscovery in 1961–2 of the overlooked palace site at Zakros (see p42). The main clue to its existence was the natural harbour, as Platon suspected the site had once been an important trading city.

**Zakros, rediscovered by Platon**

## THE DISCOVERY OF KNOSSOS

Sir Arthur Evans was inspired to dig at Knossos by the great German archaeologist Heinrich Schliemann, whose inability to purchase the site prevented him from excavating what he was convinced was a major Minoan palace. Evans, who excavated the long-lost Minoan palace at Knossos between 1900 and 1931, stands accused by some

**Colourful fresco of water carriers**

archaeologists of an excessively speculative reconstruction of the site, especially the upper floor which he dubbed the "Piano Nobile". Evans was attempting to bring to life an initially obscure and mysterious site, and his guesswork is perhaps excusable. Less admirable is the arbitrary placing of the brightly coloured "Minoan" frescoes, which are in fact 20th-century re-creations by Piet de Jong and Emile Gilliéron, some of them based on mere fragments of the original paintings.

# ⭐ Heraklion

A massive medieval fortress still guards the harbour where the galleys of the Serene Republic of Venice once moored. Centuries-old churches and ornate fountains are other reminders of Heraklion's Venetian era. Busy open-air markets and the island's most fascinating museum are also attractions. Find a café table on one of the central squares and watch the busy everyday life of a Greek city, or browse the markets for Cretan handicrafts and delicacies to take home.

### ① Morosini Fountain
Carved stone lions, the symbol of St Mark, decorate a fountain **(below)** in the hub of Heraklion's old quarter. The fountain is named after a late 17th-century doge of Venice.

**Heraklion**

### ② Venetian Fortress (Koules)
The massive walls of the square fortress **(below)** were strengthened by the Venetians as the Ottoman threat grew during the 16th century.

### ③ Archaeological Museum of Heraklion
This archaeological museum *(see pp18–19)* has an unrivalled collection from ancient Minoan, Greek and Roman cities.

### ④ Natural History Museum
This museum offers an impression of the Cretan landscape in Minoan times, before the importation of tamarisks, eucalyptus and bougainvillea. There are also stuffed animals, fossils and crystals.

### ⑦ Venetian Arsenals

The great wooden war galleys that gave Venice its maritime supremacy were built and repaired in vaulted arcades on the harbourfront opposite the fortress. Wooden fishing boats are still hauled up here for regular maintenance.

### ⑤ Venetian Bastions

Heraklion's Venetian walls **(above)** are surprisingly intact, though among a tide of modern buildings. Admire them from outside the Chania Gate, with its elaborate carving. Next to it is the Pantokratoros Bastion.

### ⑧ Agios Titos

A church dedicated to St Titus, the first bishop of Crete, has been on this site since the 10th century. The present structure **(below)** dates from the 1800s. Both church and saint are cherished by locals, as Titus is the patron of Crete.

**HERAKLION'S STORY**

The Andalucian Arabs who occupied Crete between 824 and 961 built a stronghold on the site of an earlier Roman settlement named Heracleum after the Greek hero Herakles (Hercules). Byzantine ruler Nikephoros Phokas renamed it Handax, which became Venetian Candia, then Ottoman Kandiye, while Cretan Orthodox dubbed it Megalo Kastro. Heraklion, so renamed from 1913, was bombed during World War II, but became Crete's capital in 1971.

### ⑨ Market

The old market has striped awnings and counters piled high with everything from live snails to myriad varieties of Greek olives.

### ⑩ Historical Museum of Crete

This museum's proudest possessions are the only two paintings by El Greco to have been retained in the artist's native Crete. There are also some lovely stone pieces and traditional costumes *(see p90)*.

### ⑥ Museum of Religious Art

The world's finest collection of Cretan icons can be seen in this pretty 15th-century church. Glowing depictions of saints and martyrs, some in elaborate frames, adorn the walls. Three works by Michael Damaskinos: the *Adoration of the Magi, Last Supper*, and *Christ Appearing to the Holy Women*, are here.

**NEED TO KNOW**

**MAP K3**

*Info Point Heraklion:* Nikoforou Foka Square (Lion's Square); 2813 409777; open 8:30am–2:30pm Mon–Fri

■ To see the market on 1866 Street at its best, arrive early. It remains open all day, Monday to Saturday, but most produce traders pack up by midday.

■ Plateia Venizelou (Lion Square) is an ideal spot for a drink and a rest after a morning exploring the market and city.

# Archaeological Museum of Heraklion

**An ornate item of Minoan jewellery**

### 1 Minoan Jewellery and Helmets

Gold necklaces, pendants, rings, seals, sword hilts and helmets are among the many finds from Knossos, Phaistos and Gortys. Known for their love of beauty and refinement, the Minoans produced intricately crafted jewellery, decorated with flowers and animals, and sometimes set with semi-precious coloured stones.

### 2 Hall of Frescoes

Upstairs, the museum displays lively and colourful, but heavily retouched, Minoan frescoes from Knossos, Agia Triada and other palaces. Although notionally ancient, most of what is visible is early 20th century brushwork. Some of the most extraordinary depict bull-leaping performed by young acrobats, both male and female, who would run, grab the bull by its horns and somersault over its back. Archaeologists are still undecided as to whether this was a sport or a religious ritual.

### 3 Miniature Figures

Doll-like figurines of people and animals look like toys but are believed to have had a religious purpose as votive offerings. Most were found in mountain sanctuaries and caves, such as the Dikteon (Psychro) Cave *(see p112)*. The figures offer an important insight into contemporary fashions, along with an indication of gestures of worship.

**Display of miniature figures**

### 4 Agia Triada Sarcophagus

This elaborately painted stone coffin is adorned with depictions of animal sacrifices, a funeral

**Example of the beautiful frescoes decorating the palace at Knossos**

**The Agia Triada Sarcophagus**

### 8 Phaistos Disc

This 4,000-year-old clay disc is embossed with symbols believed to be the earliest example of a form of printing. The hieroglyphics on the disc, which was unearthed at Phaistos in 1903, are the earliest-known Minoan script. No one has yet succeeded in deciphering the full text, so its meaning remains a mystery, though some archaeologists claim to have decoded the words "goddess" and "mother".

procession, women riding chariots pulled by enslaved people and mythical beasts. It was perhaps made for a Minoan ruler.

### 5 Bull's Head Rhyton

Fashioned in the shape of a bull's head, this 16th-century BCE wine vessel is carved from black steatite stone and has a mother-of-pearl snout, gilded horns, and rock crystal eyes. It was discovered at Knossos and probably used in ritual.

**Rhyton shaped like a bull's head**

### 9 Town Mosaic

Glazed tiles, each depicting multi-storey buildings of the Minoan era, were originally part of a mural decoration that may have graced the wall of a palace.

### 10 Gaming Board

A decorative gaming board, elaborately inlaid and decorated with rock crystal, gold and silver leaf, turquoise paste and ivory, shows that ancient Crete had a wealthy, leisured class, as well as trade links with other ancient civilizations.

### 6 Faience Figurines of the Snake Goddess

Unearthed at Knossos, these ornate ceramic figures display bare breasts, small waists and long flouncy skirts, and they carry a snake in either hand, as do some later depictions of the goddess Astarte. This has led some to suggest that there is continuity between ancient Crete and later Hellenic cultures. The figurines were discovered by Sir Arthur Evans *(see p14)*, who considered them as possible evidence of a matriarchal society.

### 7 Jug of Reeds

With its dark pattern of reeds painted on a lighter background, this graceful pottery jug is the finest example of work from the New Palace era (1700–1450 BCE).

**An ancient, ornate gaming board**

# TOP 10 ⭐ Chania

Chania is Crete's prettiest (and second-largest) town, with colourful old Venetian buildings set around a sheltered harbour that is guarded by fortifications. To the south are the treeless peaks of the Lefka Ori (White Mountains), sometimes snow-covered until June. Good beaches lie to the west and on the Akrotiri peninsula to the east. As well as Venetian ramparts and churches, a handful of old Islamic buildings serve as reminders of the 267-year Ottoman rule.

### 1 Lighthouse

Walk out to the lighthouse at the tip of the Venetian harbour wall **(below)** for a fine view of the waterfront, harbour entrance and city.

Chania

### 3 Byzantine Collection

The collection, which rests in a 15th-century Venetian church, highlights Byzantine Crete, with coins, jewellery, statuary, mosaics and some fine icons.

### 4 Schiavo Bastion and Venetian Walls

The massive Schiavo Bastion and the high walls either side of it are the best-preserved elements of the landward section of the Venetian fortifications. They were built in the mid-15th century as the threat of Ottoman invasion loomed.

### 2 Yali Tzami

The Turks transformed this multi-domed mosque **(below)** to set their stamp on Crete after the conquest of 1645. The oldest Ottoman building on the island (also known as the Shore Mosque), it is now a gallery.

### 5 Cretan House Folklore Museum

With its fascinating collection of tools, looms and spinning wheels, plus colourful rugs, wall hangings and ornate embroidery, this lovely museum *(see p51)* seeks to reveal and preserve traditional Cretan village skills.

### 6 Etz Hayyim Synagogue

Chania's Jewish population used this 15th-century synagogue **(left)** until the German occupation of 1941–45, when they were deported to death camps. A plaque bears the names of the 276 Jews who died when a deportees' ship was inadvertently sunk by a British submarine.

### 7 Chania Archaeological Museum

The excellent collection here includes Classical and Hellenistic sculpture *(see p49)* and glassware, Minoan pottery and clay tablets, and some fine mosaics.

**CHANIA'S STORY**

The first settlers were Minoans, who founded a powerful city named Kydonia on this site. The Romans overcame local resistance in 69 BCE, and ruled from Kastelli hill. From 1252 until 1645, Chania mainly belonged to the Venetians. It fell to the Ottomans in 1645 and they remained until 1898. During World War II, civilians fought alongside Greek and Common-wealth troops.

### 10 Iguana Beach, Agoi Apostoli

Between the Chrissi Akti headland and Glaros Beach, about 5 km (3 miles) west of the city centre, this is the best beach near Chania, with its long curve of sand and shallow waters. There are cafés and taverns nearby.

### 8 Municipal Market

This covered market **(above)** is best visited first thing in the morning. Local farm produce is piled high, and there is every imaginable variety of olive, herb and spice.

### 9 Firkas Fortress

Built to guard Chania harbour, this massive bastion now has an eclectic Naval Museum *(see p104)*, including a display depicting the Battle of Crete.

**NEED TO KNOW**

**MAP D2**

*Visitor Information:* inside the town hall at Kydonias 29; 28213 41666; open 8:30am–2:30pm Mon–Sat

*Museums:* open Wed–Mon

*Municipal Market:* closed until further notice

*Firkas Fortress:* open daily

■ Chania is a great shopping centre. For beachwear and jewellery head to Chalidon Street and the harbour. Cretan-style leather boots are found in cobblers' shops on Skridlof.

■ The priciest spots line the harbour esplanade. Try the streets of Splantzia district, for cheaper food.

# 🔟⭐ Phaistos

While Sir Arthur Evans was reconstructing Knossos, the more scientific Italian scholar Federico Halbherr was unearthing the sites of two Minoan palaces at Phaistos, on a hilltop above the farmlands of the Messara Plain. Most of the ruins visible today are remnants of a later palace (known as the Second Palace), built around 1600 BCE and destroyed, possibly by a tidal wave, around 1450 BCE.

## ① Royal Apartments

Now fenced off, these rooms – the Queen's and the King's chambers, a covered pool, and even a bathroom and lavatory with running water – were the grandest in the complex **(below)**.

## ② Grand Stairway

This broad stairway, the palace's main entrance, leads from the West Courtyard to the remains of a portico and into a colonnaded lightwell.

The ruins of the Minoan palace at Phaistos

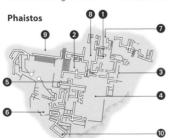

**Phaistos**

## ③ Palace Workshops

The remains of a bronzesmith's furnace or kiln stand in a courtyard. Nearby are small chambers – possibly workshops for the palace artisans.

## ④ Central Court

This vast courtyard, formerly flanked by covered walkways, may have been a parade ground. Niches, perhaps for sentries, are recessed into walls by the main entrance.

*Previous pages* Chania's multi-domed mosque as seen from the harbour

### 8 Peristyle Hall

The stumps of columns lining this square space indicate that it was once a colonnaded courtyard. Beneath it are traces of an even more archaic building, dating from what is known as the Prepalatial period (3000–1900 BCE).

### MINOAN DEMISE

There are many theories behind the sudden collapse of the Minoan civilization. Some believe it was the eruption of the volcano on the island of Kalliste (now Santorini), which would have triggered great tidal waves and clouds of volcanic ash. Other explanations include invasion by the warlike Mycenaeans of the mainland. However, all such theories remain speculative for now.

### 5 Storerooms and Pithoi

The storerooms were where essentials such as grain, oil, wine and olives were kept in huge ceramic jars **(above)** called *pithoi*. Several *pithoi* remain on display.

### 6 First Palace Remains

To the southeast of the site, the smaller ruins of the First Palace are fenced off for their protection. The palace was built c.1900 BCE and destroyed about 200 years later.

### 7 Archive

This neat row of mud-brick coffers may have been the filing department. This is where the Phaistos Disc, with its undeciphered hieroglyphics, was discovered. It is now on display in the Archaeological Museum of Heraklion *(see pp18–19)*.

### 9 West Courtyard and Theatre Area

Several tiers of stone seats **(below)** occupy the north side of the West Courtyard, a paved space by the Minoans that was used for rituals and theatrical ceremonies, including, perhaps, the bull-vaulting depicted in some Minoan frescoes. South of the courtyard are two well-like stone-lined pits that were used for storing grain, and in the northeast corner are the remains of a shrine which was part of the earlier palace.

### 10 Classical Temple

The remnants of a small temple built during the Classical period and thought to be dedicated to Rhea, the mother of Zeus, provide evidence that the site at Phaistos was still inhabited more than 1,000 years after the mysterious collapse of the Minoan civilization about 3,500 years ago.

**NEED TO KNOW**

**MAP H5** ■ 8 km (5 miles) W of Moires village ■ 28920 42315

**Open** 8am–8pm daily; last adm 7:45pm; (winter: 8am–5pm); closed some national holidays

Adm €8; Agia Triada free

■ The on-site Tourist Pavilion at Phaistos serves a range of cold drinks and food. However, you will find a better taverna in the nearby village of Vori: Alekos Taverna, beside Agia Pelagia church.

■ For an overnight stop, head for the little resort of Matala *(see p93)*, known for its sandy beaches lined with shady trees. It is less than 30 minutes' drive from Phaistos.

■ Both Phaistos and the Roman-era Gortys, a 20 minutes' drive from Phaistos, can be easily explored in a day.

# 🔟 ⭐ Rethymno

Rethymno, Crete's third-largest town, has been occupied since Minoan times and flourished under Venetian rule. Built on a wide, shallow bay, it has a good beach at the heart of town, and a medieval quarter crammed with the tall windows and wrought-iron balconies of old Venetian and Ottoman houses. Rethymno has many Orthodox and Catholic churches and mosques, which reflect the town's history of diverse cultures and religions.

### Venetian Fortress (Fortezza) ❶

Completed in 1580, this imposing stronghold **(right)** – one of the largest Venetian castles *(see p47)* ever built – broods on a headland above the town. Within the walls, the most interesting building is the Ibrahim Han Mosque, which was originally the Venetian Cathedral.

### NEED TO KNOW

**MAP F3**

*Visitor Information:* Delfini Building, 20 El. Venizelou; 28310 29148; open 8am–3pm Mon–Fri

*Fortress:* open 8:30am–8:30pm in summer; call 28310 28101 for winter hours; adm €4, family ticket €10, over 65s €3, children, students and disabled visitors free

*Museums:* Archaeological: open Wed–Mon; Folklore: open Apr–Oct: Mon–Sat

▪ Visit Rethymno early in July for the Cretan Diet Festival held in the Municipal Gardens.

▪ The harbour front caters exclusively for tourists. Head to the old quarter's quieter alleys for cheaper, less crowded and more authentically Cretan restaurants.

### ❷ Beach

Rethymno's town beach starts just east of the main harbour breakwater. Behind it is an esplanade lined with palm trees and an almost continuous chain of open-air cafés and restaurants.

### Nerantzes Mosque (Odeion) ❸

This Venetian church, now a conservatory **(right)**, was converted into a mosque by the Ottomans, who replaced the roof with cupolas and the bell tower with a balconied minaret. Today, the minaret is a true landmark in Rethymno.

### ❹ Municipal Gardens

In summer, these gardens are a good place to escape the heat. The remains of an old Muslim cemetery here were covered by the gardens in 1924.

### 5 Rimondi Fountain

This fountain **(above)** was built in 1626 by one of Rethymno's patrician families. Both Venetians and Ottomans endowed cities with public fountains.

### 8 Rethymno Archaeological Museum

Opposite the main gate of the fortress, set in a converted Ottoman ravelin which served as the local jail until 1970, is the archaeological museum *(see p49)*. Its displays **(below)** include finds from Neolithic, Minoan and Roman sites.

**MUSLIMS AND HAJIS**

Rethymno's many Islamic features reflect its Ottoman past. Until Crete gained autonomy in 1898, it had a large Muslim population. Many were later forced to migrate to Turkey under a population exchange. The Cretan name prefix "Hadzi" is a reminder of that era, indicating a Cretan who had made the pilgrimage ("Haj" in Turkish/Arabic) to the Holy Land.

Rethymno

### 6 Venetian Loggia

The most important architectural reminder of Venice's long reign is now a shop selling museum-grade reproductions of Classical works of art.

### 7 Venetian Gate (Porta Guora)

The only remnant of the city's Venetian fortifications is an arched stone gate, leading from the picturesque old quarter into the modern part of the city. Other gates were dismantled.

### 9 Inner Harbour

Situated below the Venetian Fortress, Rethymno's small inner harbour is one of the most picturesque in Greece, with ramshackle old houses, small boats at anchor and a busy quayside **(below)**.

### 10 Historical and Folk Art Museum

Vivid woven rugs and hangings, fine lace, traditional pottery, and silver and amber jewellery are among the relics of a vanished way of life preserved in this small museum *(see p50)*. Richly decorated textiles from the Franzeskaki collection are displayed.

# TOP 10 ⭐ Gortys

The ruins of Gortys, in the middle of the fertile Messara Plain, date from a much later era than Crete's Minoan palaces. It was probably first settled by the Minoans, but flourished later during the period of the Dorian city-states in the 6th century BCE. In the 2nd century BCE, Gortys defeated its rival Phaistos to become the leading Cretan city. As impressive as Crete's other archaeological ruins but less crowded, some parts of Gortys are closed to visitors for excavation work and further research.

### Basilica of Agios Titos ①

The impressive remains of the tree-aisled basilica **(right)** indicate that Christianity was already well established on the island by the 5th century, when the basilica was built. It is named after St Titus (Agios Titos), who welcomed St Paul the Apostle to Crete in 59 CE and became the first bishop of Crete.

### Roman Odeion and Code of Laws ②

Built into the walls of a Roman odeion are a number of stone slabs inscribed with a code of laws **(above)**, dating from about 500 BCE. These tablets are now regarded by scholars as the most significant archaeological feature at the Gortys site.

### Temple of Pythian Apollo ③

Believed to have been built during the 7th century BCE, this temple had an altar added in the Hellenistic period. It was converted into a Christian church during the 2nd century CE.

### Roman Agora ④

A statue of the god of healing, Asclepius (now in the Archaeological Museum of Heraklion), was discovered here. The agora, also known as the marketplace, was the heart of any ancient Greco-Roman city.

---

**NEED TO KNOW**

**MAP J5** ■ 1 km (half a mile) from Agioi Deka
■ 28920 31144

**Open** 8am–8pm daily; last adm 7:45pm (winter: 8:30am–5pm); closed some national holidays

Adm €6; concessions €3

■ Drive to Matala, 30 km (19 miles) southwest of Gortys, which has a sandy beach *(see p60)*.

■ Instead of using the spartan on-site cafeteria at Gortys, head for the nearby village of Agioi Deka, where there are pleasant tavernas and a historic church.

**BYZANTINE GORTYS**

After the Roman conquest of 67 BCE, Gortys became capital of the Roman province of Crete and Cyrenaica (modern Libya). The Holy Ten (Agioi Deka in Greek) were martyred here in 250 CE. It continued to flourish as a provincial hub until it was sacked by Saracen raiders during the late 7th century CE. It was finally abandoned by its inhabitants in 824 CE, after another sacking by the Andalucian Arabs.

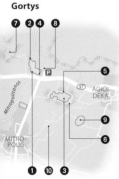

### 6 Praetorium

A courtyard and stumps of marble columns **(above)** are all that remain of the palace of the Roman governor of Crete and Libya.

### 7 Acropolis (Kastro)

Outside the main site, Roman ramparts and a small tower known as the Kastro ("castle") stand guard on a low hilltop. The site is fenced, and the worn-out path makes access difficult.

### 10 Roman Baths

Remnants of the baths, which would have been a social hub of the Roman city, can be seen among olive groves south of the Praetorium.

### 8 Museum

A collection of marble statuary unearthed at Gortys is on display in a small pavilion on site **(right)**, though many of the more impressive finds are held at the Archaeological Museum of Heraklion (see pp 18–19).

**Gortys**

### 9 Minoan Rural Villa

West of the Metropolianos stream, lie the excavated remains of a Minoan villa **(below)** with 30 rooms dating from the Neopalatial Period (1700–1450 BCE).

### 5 Temple of Isis and Serapis

Ancient Crete had links with ancient Egypt, as shown by the remains of this temple, dedicated to the Egyptian deities.

# 🔟⭐ Samaria Gorge

The Samaria Gorge, which cuts its way through the Lefka Ori (White Mountains) from the Omalos Plateau to the Libyan Sea, is one of the most striking areas of natural beauty in Greece. Peaks soar on both sides of the gorge, flanked by pine woods and wildflower meadows. Beginning 1,250 m (4,100 ft) above sea level, it emerges on the coast, close to the little village of Agia Roumeli, after passing through the narrow Sidero Portes or "Iron Gates".

### 4 Old Agia Roumeli

A ruined Venetian-era church and a few cottages are all that remain of this old village. On the left (east) bank of the gorge exit lie the ruins of ancient Tarra; up the hill, beyond the right bank sits a crumbled Ottoman fortress.

### 1 Xyloskalo

The zig zag path **(above)** down through the gorge is called the Xyloskalo. The toughest part plummets a breathtaking 1,000 m (3,280 ft) in little more than 2 km (1 mile), passing through pine and cypress woods.

### 2 Church of Agios Nikolaos

Not far from the foot of the Xyloskalo and the springs, the tiny chapel of Agios Nikolaos **(below)** stands in the shade of pine and cypress trees, next to a rest area.

### 3 Gingilos and Volakias Peaks

Above the Xyloskalo path to the southwest, the skyline is dominated by the massive peaks of Gingilos (2,080 m/ 6,824 ft) and Volakias (2,116 m/6,942 ft). It is not unusual for these mountaintops to remain snow covered well into the early summer, even when the temperatures at sea level are scorching.

**Samaria Gorge**

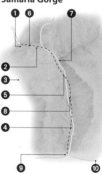

### NEED TO KNOW

**MAP C4** ■ Forest Guardhouse, Xyloskalo; 28210 67179 ■ Forest Guardhouse, Agia Roumeli; 28210 45570

**Open** May–mid-Oct (weather permitting, phone first to check): 7am–8pm daily

Adm €5; keep your date-stamped ticket, which you must hand in at the Agia Roumeli gate as you leave

■ Though fit walkers can complete the 16-km (10-mile) trek in about 5 hours, it is best to allow 8, including a break of at least an hour. Rest during the hottest part of the day in summer.

■ Take at least one litre of water per person. There are rest areas where you can picnic in the shade, and at Agia Roumeli there are several tavernas for your recuperation.

**GETTING AROUND**

Several companies run guided walks, which include transport to and from the gorge. There are also buses from Chania to Omalos, 1 km (half a mile) from Xyloskalo. Independent walkers must report to the Forest Guardhouse at Xyloskalo before setting out. There are many guesthouses in Agia Roumeli.

**(8) Osia Maria**
Dwarfed by steep cliffs, this small church contains 14th-century frescoes and lends its name to the gorge itself.

**(9) New Agia Roumeli**
The inhabitants of Agia Roumeli abandoned their village in the 1960s, intent on a new location by the sea (**below**). The modern village has a string of tavernas and guest-houses spread out along a single street.

**(5) Sidero Portes**
Near the shrine of Afendis Christos, the gorge narrows to just 3 m (9 ft) of space separating rocky walls (**above**) that rise 300 m (more than 1,000 ft).

**(6) Neroutsiko and Riza Sykias**
The bubbling springs of Neroutsiko and Riza Sykias meet at the foot of the Xyloskalo path. During winter, they form a fierce torrent that makes the gorge impassable, but in the summer months, they dry to a trickle.

**(7) Samaria**
The last dwellers in the gorge abandoned this village in 1962, when the area was designated a national park. The ghostly cottages have become ever more derelict over time.

**(10) Agios Pavlos Beach**
An hour's walk east of Agia Roumeli, Agios Pavlos beach is a long stretch of sand and pebbles with a taverna. It is named after the tiny chapel here, dedicated to St Paul.

# TOP 10 ⭐ The Amari Valley and Mount Ida

The remote Amari Valley, overlooked by Mount Ida, is one of Crete's most scenic areas, dotted with churches, olive groves and vineyards. Surprisingly fertile thanks to topsoil washed from surrounding slopes, this region was among the wealthiest in Crete in the Byzantine era. During World War II, many of its villages were destroyed by the Germans in retaliation for attacks by the resistance, and its kidnapping of General Kreipe.

**1 Thronos**
The 11th-century church of the Panagia at Thronos holds frescoes and traces of ancient mosaics. A nearby shop keeps the church keys.

**2 Moni Asomaton**
The monastery of Asomaton **(above)**, built during the Venetian era, is now deserted. It stands in an oasis of plane trees, palms and eucalyptus.

**3 Agios Ioannis Theologos**
The 13th-century church of St John the Divine sits by the road just north of Kardaki village. The frescoes date from 1347.

**4 Ideou Cave**
According to Greek myth, Zeus was raised in this enormous cavern, 20 minutes' walk from the Nida Plateau. In ancient times, this was a place of pilgrimage. Artifacts such as bronze shields, left as offerings to Zeus in the 8th century BCE, are found in the Archaeological Museum of Heraklion. The cavern is open daily.

**5 Kamares Cave**
This cave, where remarkable Minoan pottery known as Kamares ware was discovered, is a 4-hour trek from Kamares village. This sacred site was dedicated to the goddess Eileithyia.

**Panoramic view over the lush Amari Valley**

### 8 Amari Village

A Venetian clock tower **(left)** is one of the older buildings in the valley. Just outside the village, some of Crete's oldest Christian frescoes, dated 1225, are in Agia Anna church.

### 9 The Memorial to Peace

German artist Karen Raeck's work, to the north of the Nida Plateau, is a winged figure outlined in huge natural stone boulders.

**GETTING AROUND THE VALLEY**

Though the Amari Valley feels remote, there is one bus running on weekdays (Mon–Fri) from Rethymno to the region's two largest villages, Thronos and Amari. With a hired car, it is possible to drive up one side of the valley and down the other. Of the two roads going through the valley, the eastern route is the most spectacular.

**The Amari Valley and Mount Ida**

### 6 Hromonastiri

The church of Agios Efstathios, outside Hromonastiri village, contains frescoes dating from the 11th century, which may be the oldest of their kind in Crete.

### 10 Fourfouras

A pretty village set in mountain scenery, Fourfouras is one of the jumping-off spots for the ascent of Mount Ida and some of the less challenging hikes on the Psiloritis massif.

### 7 Mount Ida (Psiloritis) Summit

Towering above the valley, the 2,456-m (8,060-ft) peak of Mount Ida, also called Psiloritis, is the highest mountain **(below)** in Crete. Marked walking trails *(see p64)* lead to the top from the Nida Plateau, 23 km (14 miles) by road from Anogeia village.

**NEED TO KNOW**

MAP G4–H4
*Greek National Tourism Organization:* Delfini Building, Sofokli Venizelou, Rethymno; 28310 29148

■ Amari is a good base from which to explore the valley and surrounding mountains on foot. Alternatively, try the nearby village of Spili, directly west over the Kedros range.

■ Guided fossil-hunting and herb-gathering walks *(€30 per person)* around the Amari Valley are organized by Lambros Papoutsakis in Thronos village *(28330 22760)*. Another walk takes participants to Psiloritis summit, starting before dawn *(€50 per person)*.

# ⭐ Spinalonga

A small island off Lasithi's north coast, Spinalonga offers a window into the complex tapestry of Crete's past. Initially constructed by the Venetians in the 16th century, its fortifications have witnessed centuries of change. Surrendered to the Ottomans in 1715, the island was later home to a largely Muslim population before serving as a leper colony for which it's best known. Today, the abandoned site is home to fascinating remains of the colony, where up to 1,000 Greeks quarantined between 1903 and 1957.

## 1 Venetian Walls

The Venetians built Spinalonga's fortifications in 1574, to defend against Turkish expansion and to protect Elounda's salterns. The walls **(below)**. surrounding the island feature guard towers and symbols of the Venetian Republic.

### NEED TO KNOW

**MAP N4** ▪ 15.6 km (9.6 miles) from Agios Nikolaos ▪ (02) 8410 22462

**Open** Apr–Oct: 8:30am–6pm daily

Adm €8

▪ Boats regularly ferry tourists to Spinalonga from the ports of Plaka (*www.plakaboat.gr*) and Elounda (*www.eloundaboat.gr*) from 9am to 4:30pm at 30-minute intervals. Boat journeys to the island are dependant on weather conditions.

▪ There is a small café and a souvenir shop on the island, but the nearby town of Elounda is the best option for restaurants and bars.

## 2 Hospital Wards

Spinalonga served as Greece's foremost leprosarium, with a dedicated hospital for treating leprosy patients. Several structures offer an insight into the era's medical facilities and living conditions.

## 3 Spinalonga Museum

This museum displays artifacts from the Minoan era to the 20th century, with an exhibition of objects from the former leper colony

## 4 Dante's Gate

Upon arriving at Spinalonga's jetty, patients would walk through a 20-m-(3-ft-) long tunnel called Dante's Gate. Also known as the "Tunnel of Tears", this haunting passage marked their final link to the outside world.

### 5 Houses and Marketplace

The island's central path reveals ruins of residences, a set of steps **(right)** and a former market site, all of which provide a glimpse into life on Spinalonga. Remains of buildings are scattered all over the island.

### 7 Aloe Vera Gardens

Visitors may spot aloe vera gardens growing within some of the island's deserted homes. These medicinal plants were cultivated by the patients for their skin-soothing and therapeutic properties.

### 8 Beach

Opposite the port of Plaka lies a small stretch of beach with breathtaking views of the sea. However, swimming is strictly prohibited here due to strong currents and, more recently, boat traffic.

**THE ISLAND**

Interest in Spinalonga has increased since the publication of Victoria Hislop's *The Island* (2005), which is centred around the island's tumultuous history. In the novel, Hislop explores the lives of the inhabitants who were afflicted by leprosy, and its impact on their families. With its themes of love and resilience, the novel helped combat the stigma that persisted long after the evacuation of Spinalonga in 1957.

The island of Spinalonga

### 6 Cemetery and Ossuary

Located in a remote corner of Spinalonga, the cemetery and ossuary are a testament to the island's history, and house the remains of the patients who were interred here.

### 9 Garrison

Situated near a secondary access point used by doctors, this Venetian-era garrison played an important role as a disinfection room when the island served as a leper colony. Remarkably, disinfection equipment from this period still survives and can be viewed here.

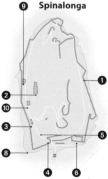

Spinalonga

### 10 Agios Paintelemonas

At the centre of the settlement lies St Panteleimon's church, with its distinctive bell **(left)**, where priests resided alongside patients. Every year, visitors make a pilgrimage here to remember their ancestors who died on the island.

# 🔟⭐ Moni Arkadi

High above Crete's north coast, on a fertile plain at the base of Mount Ida, Moni Arkadi (Arkadi Monastery) dates from the 16th century. When Crete fell under Ottoman occupation in 1669, monasteries became important centres of resistance – thanks, in part, to their isolation. Besides teaching Christian values, the monks kept alive the Greek language, and during Crete's many 18th- and 19th-century rebellions, Orthodox priests often led freedom fighters into combat. Despite Arkadi's serene atmosphere, it conceals a tragic story, and the Cretan independence movement slogan "Freedom or Death" (today the Greek national motto) holds special significance here.

### 1 Monastery Church

This Venetian-Baroque church **(right)** dates from 1587. The humble interior has walls with Cretan frescoes, two altars, golden candelabras, icons covered by silver plating (so that just the saints' faces are visible) and flickering votive candles.

### 2 Courtyard Garden

The courtyard **(below)** is lined with fragrant roses. Stone pillars support a pergola draped with vines, while terracotta pots hold geraniums and bougainvillea, and cats snooze in the shade of a cypress tree.

### 3 Museum

The monastery refectory now hosts a museum, with exhibits including ecclesiastical books and manuscripts, holy crosses, silk vestments embroidered with golden thread and religious icons. Look out for *St John the Baptist* and *Christ Enthroned*.

### 5 Gunpowder Store

This building is where, on 8 November 1866, 943 Cretan martyrs blew themselves up rather than surrender to the Ottomans. Today, a commemorative plaque reads: "The flame which lights the depths of this crypt was a Godly flame in which the Cretans perished for freedom."

### 4 Arkadi Café

Next to the memorial, the café serves drinks and snacks at tables on a shaded terrace with views over the surrounding countryside. There is also a children's playground with swings and a slide.

### 7 Monks' Cells
Throughout the 17th century, about 100 monks resided here – today there are only three left. Behind the church, you can see a couple of the former monks' cells – small and simply furnished **(left)**.

### 8 Memorial to the Dead
Outside the monastery complex, a five-minute walk brings you to a raised stone terrace shaded by pine trees. Here, inside a former windmill, hexagonal in plan, an ossuary displays the skulls of those who perished during the Arkadi Holocaust of 1866.

### 9 Outer Walls
The monastery was fortified in the 16th century to defend it against attack and to offer refuge to both the monks and the local community. Visitors can enter through the main portal, an arched gateway in the west façade, from 1870.

### THE ARKADI HOLOCAUST
On 8 November 1866, the monastery came under siege by the Ottoman army. Some 700 women and children (who had sought refuge within its walls) and over 200 Cretan freedom fighters barricaded themselves inside. Rather than surrender, they fired their store of gunpowder, blowing themselves (and many attackers) up. This act of defiance was the culmination of five revolts since 1770. Crete was finally united with Greece in 1913.

### 10 Dead Tree
As you face the church façade, you will see a cypress and an olive tree. Behind them, the dead tree **(below)** has a bullet from the 1866 siege still embedded in its trunk.

### 6 Refectory
A gate located opposite the iconic dead tree leads into a second – smaller and more peaceful – courtyard. Cross this space to arrive at the refectory, a long, narrow space with a vaulted ceiling. The monks would dine together here, sitting at communal wooden tables.

**NEED TO KNOW**

**MAP G4** ■ Arkadi, 23 km (14 miles) SE of Rethymno ■ 28310 83135

**Open** 9am–8pm daily (Apr, May & Sep: to 7pm, Oct & Mar: to 6pm, Nov & Dec: to 5pm); Adm €3

■ Buses depart daily from Rethymno KTEL *(10am & 1pm, returning 12:15pm & 3:15pm; journey time 40 mins)*. Alternatively, a miniature train follows the same route.

■ On 8 November each year, a 1-minute silence is held at the monastery to mark the Arkadi Holocaust, and a commemorative ceremony takes place in the monastery church.

■ The neighbouring ossuary holds the skulls of the victims of the massacre as a grisly memento mori.

# The Top 10 of Everything

**Vibrant mural decorations inside the palace of Knossos**

# 🔟 Moments in History

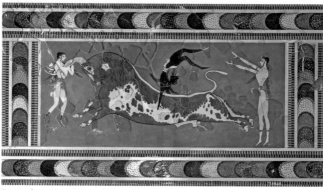

**Fresco from the palace of Knossos showing an acrobat leaping over a bull**

## 1 1750 BCE: Minoan Culture Thrives

Crete is the centre of the Minoan civilization, which is marked by the building of Knossos and other grand palaces. Mycenaeans take over Knossos shortly after 1450 BCE.

## 2 Roman Conquest

The first Roman invasion of Crete in 71 BCE is repulsed by the Dorian Greeks, but a second attack in 69 BCE succeeds. Some Cretan cities side with the invaders, and by 67 BCE, Crete is firmly in Roman hands.

## 3 Byzantine Reconquest

The Byzantine Empire loses Crete to Arab invaders in 824 CE.

**General Nikephoros Phokas**

Just over a century later, in 961, general Nikephoros Phokas reconquers the island.

## 4 Venetian Rule

Crete falls into Venetian hands shortly after 1204, when the Fourth Crusade goes awry and the Byzantine emperor is deposed by an army of Frankish crusaders in alliance with Venice. Cretans rebel against the Venetians, but without success.

## 5 The Ottoman Turks

Chania and Rethymno fall to an attack by Turks in 1645. Venetian sea power enables the Venetian capital of Candia (modern Heraklion) to resist a 21-year siege, but Venice finally surrenders in 1669.

## 6 Rebellions Against Ottoman Rule

Shipbuilder Ioannis Daskalogiannis leads Crete's first revolt against Ottoman rule in 1770. It is crushed, as is the 1828 rebellion led by the revolutionary leader Chatzimichalis Dalianis. Subsequent failures in 1841 and 1858 are followed by the great rising of 1866, when a self-appointed Cretan Assembly declares union (*enosis*) with Greece. The rising is brutally quelled, but it arouses international sympathy for the Cretan cause.

### 7 Great Powers Intervene

Further revolts in 1889 and 1896 culminate in the landing of Greek troops in 1897 as well as intervention by France, Britain, Russia and Italy. Crete becomes semi-autonomous, ruled by a Christian-Muslim assembly, chaired by Prince George of Greece.

### 8 Union with Greece

In 1905, local politician Eleftherios Venizelos convenes a revolutionary assembly, which in 1908 unilaterally declares *enosis* (union) with Greece. This does not occur until 1913.

### 9 Occupation and Liberation in World War II

German forces drive the Allies out of Crete in May 1941, but Cretan guerrillas continue to resist. Most German troops flee Greece in October 1944 as Allied troops land, but the garrison at Chania holds out until Berlin falls in May 1945.

**Occupation of Crete by German forces**

### 10 Earthquakes Strike Crete

Two strong 6-magnitude earthquakes strike Crete in September and October 2021. The largest earthquakes experienced by the island in 60 years, the tremors cause one fatality, several injuries and widespread damage to older buildings in southeastern Crete.

---

**TOP 10 EMPIRES AND GOVERNMENTS**

**Picture of an Ottoman seige**

**1 Minoan Empires**
The Minoan civilization emerged between 3000 and 1900 BCE. A volcanic explosion may have destroyed the Minoan cities around 1450 BCE.

**2 Mycenaeans**
Myceanean Greeks from the mainland settled in Crete after 1450 BCE.

**3 The Dorians**
During the 1100s, Dorian Greeks from northern Greece drove the descendants of the Minoans into remote areas.

**4 Dorian City-States**
Gortys and Kydonia (modern Chania) were among the most powerful.

**5 Roman Empire**
Gortys (which had sided with invading Rome) became capital of the province of Crete and Cyrenaica.

**6 Byzantine Empire**
In the 4th century CE, Crete became part of the Byzantine realm.

**7 Arab Conquest and Retreat**
From 824–961 CE, Arab forces led by the Andalucian Abu Hafs occupied Crete; Byzantine general Nikephoros Phokas expelled them.

**8 Venetian Empire**
In 1210, the Republic of Venice took control of Crete in the wake of the Fourth Crusade.

**9 Ottoman Empire**
The Ottoman Turks invaded Crete in strength in 1645 and held the island until the end of the 19th century.

**10 Kingdom of the Hellenes**
Crete was united with Greece in 1913. From 1898 to 1923, around 100,000 Muslim Cretans voluntarily departed, or were expelled.

# TOP 10 Ancient Sites

## 1 Itanos
MAP R4 ■ 2 km (1 mile) N of Vai ■ Unenclosed

The remains of a Hellenistic wall, foundations of two early Christian basilicas, and toppled columns are the only indications that this was once an important city. It flourished until early medieval times, when it was destroyed by Saracen raiders.

**Ruins of the basilica, Itanos**

## 2 Gournia
MAP P5 ■ S of coast road, 18 km (11 miles) E of Agios Nikolaos ■ 28420 93028 ■ Open 8am–3pm Tue–Sun ■ Adm

The well-preserved remains of the Minoan town of Gournia, a maze of roofless stone walls, makes an interesting contrast with the better-known Minoan palaces. This was a working community, and archaeologists discovered workshops used by potters, smiths and carpenters, alongside tiny houses surrounding a small palace.

## 3 Agia Triada
A treasury of Minoan relics, including tablets inscribed with the still undeciphered Minoan Linear A script, has been discovered on this site (see p90) of a Minoan villa, built about 1700 BCE. The site was later occupied by Mycenaean settlers, who built a *megaron* (chief's hall) and a village.

## 4 Malia
MAP M4 ■ 3 km (2 miles) E of Malia ■ 28970 31597 ■ Open 8am–5pm Tue–Sun ■ Adm

East of the busy summer holiday resort of Malia is the archaeological site of the same name. The Minoan double-axe symbol, or *labrys*, is carved into two pillars of a small shrine, which forms part of the remains of a palace dating circa 1600 BCE. Excavations are still going on near the palace site.

## 5 Zakros
MAP R5 ■ Kato Zakros ■ 28430 26897 ■ Open 8am–6pm daily ■ Adm

The fourth-largest of Crete's Minoan palaces, Zakros was rediscovered in 1961 by the Cretan archaeologist Nikolaos Platon. The site had not been plundered, and finds included a stunning rock crystal jug, which is today housed in the Archaeological Museum of Heraklion (see pp18–19).

### 6 Praisos
**MAP Q5 ■ By Nea Praisos village ■ Unenclosed**

This scenic site – with only the remnants of a temple, house foundations and a city wall to be seen – was the last enclave of the Eteocretan ("true Cretan") descendants of the Minoans. It survived until the 2nd century BCE.

### 7 Ancient Eleftherna

Eleftherna, about 30 km (19 miles) from Rethymno, is one of Crete's most important settlement sites *(see p104)*. Inhabited from prehistoric times until the early Christian era, the site features ruins of cemeteries, sanctuaries, an aqueduct and Roman roads. Findings are kept in the Archaeological Site Museum of Ancient Eleftherna.

### 8 Phaistos

The ruins of the Minoan palace at Phaistos *(see pp24–5)*, on a hilltop by the south coast of Crete, are second only to those at Knossos. A maze of walls and courtyards marks the site of the Second Palace at Phaistos, built around 1600 BC. Hieroglyphics on the clay Phaistos Disc still puzzle scientists today.

**Remains of the basilica at Gortys**

### 9 Gortys

The ruined city of Gortys *(see pp28–9)*, with the basilica of Agios Titos and remnants of a Roman provincial governor's palace, dates from the early Christian era. The site extends over quite a wide area, and is usually uncrowded, so it can be explored at leisure.

**The Phaistos Disc, carved with symbols**

### 10 Knossos

Just outside Heraklion, Knossos *(see pp12–15)* is by far the most striking of the Minoan palace ruins on Crete. Dating back more than 3,500 years, it was destroyed in around 1450 BCE, probably by a combination of volcanic eruption and invaders, and not redis-covered until the late 19th century.

**The imposing palace of Knossos**

# ⭐10 Churches and Monasteries

**Interior of Panagia Kera at Krista**

### 1 Panagia Kera
**MAP N5** ■ 28410 51525
■ Open 8am–3pm Tue–Sun ■ Adm

Crete's main Byzantine-era church, Panagia Kera was built in the 13th and 14th centuries. It is adorned with vivid, unusual frescoes, many of them from the apocryphal gospels, as well as a rare Orthodox depiction of Catholic saint Francis.

### 2 Moni Preveli
**MAP F5** ■ 28320 31246
■ Open 9am–6:30pm daily ■ Adm

Built during the 17th century, Moni Piso Preveli's cells overlook a broad, open courtyard to the Libyan sea. It has a church and a small museum where exhibits include ornamented vestments, church silver and icons. Kato Preveli (same hours and admission) is also worth visiting for its older architecture and another museum.

### 3 Agia Pelagia
Open access

This tiny 14th-century church, well-signposted near the top of this village, has quirky frescoes of the life of Christ such as *His Presentation to the Crucifixion*, as well as assorted saints and even musicians.

### 4 Agios Nikolaos
**MAP D2** ■ Open 8am–7pm daily

This church has a history that reflects Chania's past. It was built by the Venetians, converted into a mosque after the Ottoman conquest, and in the early 20th century, it was converted again into a Greek Orthodox church dedicated to St Nicholas. Its minaret is a relic from the centuries of Muslim worship here.

### 5 Moni Arkadi

Though founded in the 5th century, most of this monastic complex dates from the 16th century. Moni Arkadi (see pp36–7) has a special meaning for Cretans. During the great revolt of 1866, the monastery was besieged by the Ottomans. Rather than surrender, the rebel defenders blew up their gunpowder stores, killing themselves and many of their enemies.

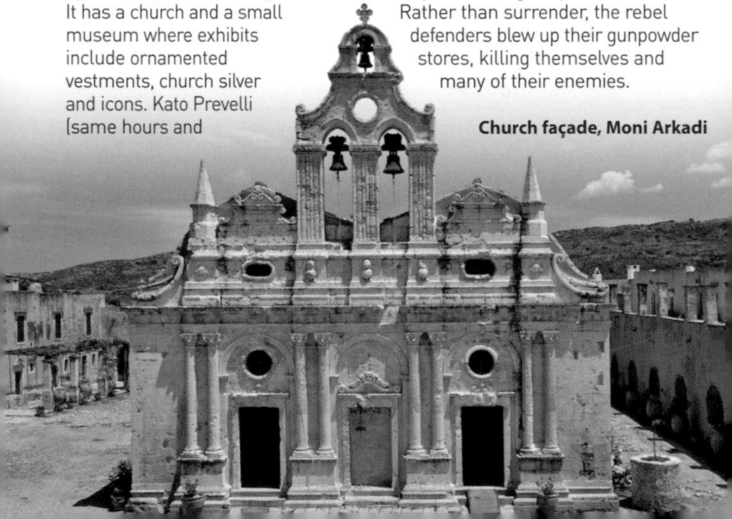

**Church façade, Moni Arkadi**

*Sea of Crete*

### 6 Moni Chrissopygi
MAP D2 ▪ 28210 91125 ▪ Open 8am–noon & 3:30–6pm daily ▪ Adm

The Convent of the Golden Font (Life-Giving Spring), dates from the late Venetian era but has been rebuilt many times, most recently in 1976. The nuns paint icons using traditional methods.

**Byzantine icon at Moni Toplou**

### 7 Moni Toplou
MAP R4 ▪ 28430 61226 ▪ Open 9am–1pm & 2–6pm daily ▪ Adm

Fortified against bandits at its 14th-century foundation, Toplou monastery features a forbidding exterior. Inside, however, is a different world of serene, flower-filled courtyards and cloisters, and a church that houses the icon *Lord, Thou Art Great* by Ioannis Kornaros.

### 8 Agioi Deka Church
MAP J5 ▪ Open 8am–5pm daily

This 13th-century Byzantine Church of the Ten Saints stands on the spot where ten Cretan Christians were martyred by the troops of the Roman Emperor Decius in 250 CE. A striking icon depicting the ten saints with golden halos is displayed in the nave.

### 9 Moni Katholiko
MAP D2 ▪ Open access

In a valley riddled with caves once used by hermits, the abandoned monastery of Katholiko is a ghostly place, with crumbling buildings that seem to have grown out of the rock face.

### 10 Moni Agia Triada Tzangarolon
MAP D2 ▪ 28210 63572 ▪ 9am–7pm daily (Museum Hall closed Sun) ▪ Adm

Tzangarolon monastery stands among its own olive groves. Although its monastic community has dwindled to just a few members, its old buildings are gradually being restored and its church exterior vies with Arkadi for ornateness. Visitors are welcome, and the monks will sell you high-quality, home-grown olive oil and wine.

**Iconostasis at Moni Agia Triada**

# 🔟 Venetian Castles

### 1 Frangokastello
**MAP E4**

The Venetians built this fortress (see p102) to defend the south coast from Saracen pirates. In May 1828 it was occupied by Greek insurgents, who were massacred by a much larger Muslim force. Yearly, around the battle anniversary, legend has it that the defeated appear as phantoms marching out of nearby sand dunes (see p55). The repaired castle hosts summer events.

**The coastal fortress of Frangokastello**

### 2 Venetian Tower, Finikas, Loutro
**MAP D4**

The lonely tower, standing on a headland between Loutro and the bay of Finix, is yet another Venetian relic. Nearby are a few scattered blocks, the remains of a Byzantine church and also a Hellenistic town, the latter an important seaport when the Romans ruled Crete.

### 3 Chania
**MAP D2**

The Venetians lost Chania to their arch-rivals, the Genoese, in 1263. They regained it 22 years later, and set about making the town impregnable, starting with walls around the hill above the harbour in the district still known as Kastelli (the castle). Further walls followed, but though they may have deterred occasional pirate raids, they proved entirely ineffective when the Ottomans assailed the city in 1645.

### 4 Paleochora
**MAP B4**

Kastel Selinou, as Paleochora was first known, was built in 1279 to guard the southwest against pirates. The great Muslim corsair Barbarossa destroyed it in 1539. The Ottomans saw no need to rebuild it, and Paleochora fort has remained an elegant ruin ever since.

### 5 Da Molini Castle Ruins, Alikianos
**MAP C2**

Though much overgrown, the dilapidated walls standing among clutches of citrus trees are still impressive. The castle was the scene of a notorious massacre, when the early 16th-century Cretan rebel leader Georgios Kandanoleon was betrayed by Francesco Molini during his son's wedding to Molini's daughter.

**Sitia's magnificent Venetian fortress**

### 6 Venetian Fortress, Sitia
**MAP Q4**

This restored fort is all that remains of the city's once substantial ring of battlements, which resisted a siege by the Ottomans in 1648–51. It is now used as an open-air theatre for concerts and plays in summer.

### 7 Gramvousa
**MAP B1**

In around 1220, the Venetians built a strong fortress on this tiny islet off northwestern Crete, and – along with fortified Spinalonga and Souda islets – held it until 1715, long after they had lost Crete itself. Boat excursions are available from Kissamos.

### 8 Acropolis and Ancient Polyrrinia
**MAP B2**

On a hilltop above the modern village of Polyrrinia, a keep shares the peak with the ruins of Hellenistic Polyrrinia, which thrived until the Andalucian Arab invasion of the 9th century. Stone from Hellenistic buildings, already 1,000 years old when the Venetians arrived, can still be seen here.

### 9 Rethymno Fortezza

The massive fortress (see p26) that dominates Rethymno's harbour was built by the Venetians with sloping walls to better deflect the Ottoman Empire's gigantic cannon. But it proved no match for the military ingenuity of the Ottomans, who simply skirted it when they took the city in 1645. The Fortezza never again had a military function, and until the early 20th century many houses nestled within.

**The mosque inside Rethymno's Fortezza**

### 10 Spinalonga

This formidable island fortress was built in 1579 to command the entrance to the Gulf of Mirabello. Venice managed to keep it after the surrender of Candia (Heraklion) in 1669, and relinquished it by treaty in 1715. From 1903 to 1957, it was used as a leper colony (see pp34–5), as told in Victoria Hislop's novel The Island.

**The fortress of Spinalonga, overlooking Elounda Bay**

# 🔟 Art and Archaeological Museums

### ① Archanes Collection
MAP K4 ▪ Kalochristianaki, Archanes ▪ 2810 752712 ▪ Open summer: 8:30am–2:30pm Wed–Mon

Finds from the Minoan cemetery discovered at Fourni, just north of Archanes village, are displayed in this small archaeological museum, along with relics from other nearby sites.

### ② Museum of Contemporary Art of Crete, Rethymno
MAP F3 ▪ Mesolongiou 32, Rethymno 74131 ▪ 28310 52530 ▪ Open 9am–2pm & 7–9pm Tue–Fri, 10am–3pm Sat & Sun ▪ Adm

This museum has around 500 works by local artist L Kanakakis, as well as works by other leading, contemporary Greek artists. The pieces range from the 1950s to the present day. It also holds temporary exhibitions, as well as classes and workshops, open to the public.

### ③ Archaeological Museum of Heraklion
Besides its famous Minoan exhibits (see pp18–19), the collection here has significant Roman-era finds.

### ④ Historical Museum of Crete
MAP S1 ▪ Sofokli Venizelou 27, Heraklion ▪ 2810 283219 ▪ Open 9am–5pm Mon–Sat ▪ Adm

Wonderfully eclectic displays include an interactive model of the medieval town, two genuine El Grecos, rescued icons and frescoes, as well as antiquarian prints from World War II and the city of Heraklion.

**Statuette, Archaeological Museum of Heraklion**

### ⑤ Archaeological Museum of Kissamos
MAP B2 ▪ Plateia Tzanaki ▪ 28220 83308 ▪ Open 8:30am–3:30pm Wed–Mon ▪ Adm

Housed in a fine Venetian-Turkish building, this museum displays Hellenistic and Roman artifacts, including jewellery, statues and two exquisite mosaic floors.

**Floor mosaic in the Archaeological Museum of Kissamos**

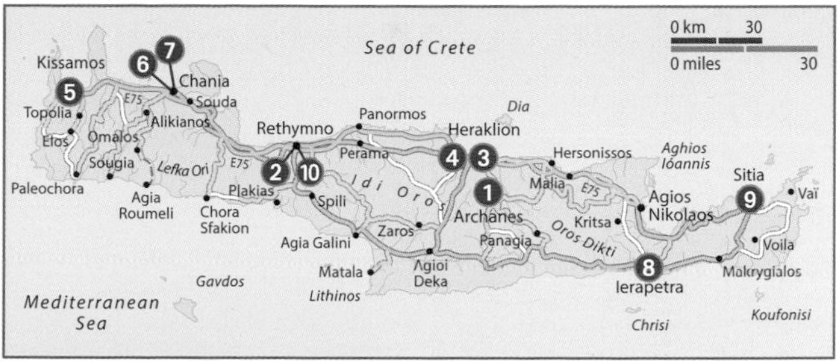

**Chania Archaeological Museum**

### 8 Ierapetra Archaeological Museum

MAP N6 ▪ 1 Kostoula Adrianou Ierapetra ▪ 28420 28721 ▪ Open 8am–3pm Wed–Sun ▪ Adm

Exhibits inside this former Muslim academy include huge clay storage jars (pithoi), Minoan clay sarcophagi (larnakes) statues, bronze weapons and tools dating from the time of the Dorian city-states, when Ierapetra became one of the most powerful cities in eastern Crete.

### 6 Archaeological Museum of Chania

MAP B6 ▪ 28210 90334 ▪ Open Apr–Oct: 8am–9pm Wed–Mon; Nov–Mar: 9am–4pm Wed–Mon ▪ Adm

Set in an iconic modern building facing the sea, this museum is filled with Minoan finds, Roman and Hellenistic sculptures, pottery and jewellery found at archaeological sites in western Crete.

### 9 Archaeological Museum of Sitia

MAP Q4 ▪ Fiskokefalou 3 ▪ 28430 23917 ▪ Open 8:30am–3:30pm Wed–Mon ▪ Adm

The main exhibits are from the palace site at Zakros, which was uncovered in 1961. They include clay tablets inscribed with the symbols of the Minoan Linear, A script, as well as bronze and kitchen tools.

### 7 Byzantine Collection of Chania

MAP A5 ▪ 78 Theotoko poulou ▪ 28210 96046 ▪ Open 8:30am–3:30pm Wed–Mon ▪ Adm

The fine collection of Cretan icons is the best reason to visit this small museum next to Chania's harbour fortress, housed in the Venetian church of San Salvatore. The collection also features a floor mosaic, fresco fragments rescued from country chapels, jewellery, ceramics and coins.

**Vase, Sitia Archaeological Museum**

### 10 Archaeological Museum of Rethymno

MAP P2 ▪ Agios Frangiskos 4 ▪ 28310 27506 ▪ Open 10am–6pm Wed–Mon ▪ Adm ▪ www.archmuseum.gr

This museum's collection stretches from the Stone Age to Minoan and Hellenistic eras. Exhibits include late Minoan painted burial caskets, or larnakes, and goods from cemetery sites. The museum is temporarily housed in a former church.

# 🔟 Cretan Cultural Museums

**Lychnostatis Open Air Museum**

## 1 Lychnostatis Open Air Museum of Folk Culture

MAP M4 ■ Hersonissos ■ 28970 23660 ■ Open Apr–Nov: 9am–2pm Sun–Fri; winter: visits by appt ■ Adm ■ www.lychnostatis.gr

Traditional Cretan ways of life began to die out in recent decades. This open-air museum gives some insight into life on the island before tourism, TVs and mobile phones. Exhibits include a windmill and an old stone cottage.

## 2 Historical and Folk Art Museum, Rethymno

MAP P2 ■ Vernardou 28-30 ■ 28310 23398 ■ Open 10am–2:30pm Mon–Sat; may close Nov–Mar ■ Adm

This converted Venetian mansion displays relics of a vanished way of life, including colourful woven artifacts, embroidery, farm and kitchen implements, and ceramics.

## 3 Olive Tree Museum, Vouves

MAP C2 ■ Ano Vouves (30 km/19 miles W of Chania) ■ Open 10am–7pm

Set amid olive groves, with one tree said to be 3,000 years old, this quaint museum traces the history of olive oil. Exhibits include an old press and terracotta pots. The adjoining café serves delicious cakes.

## 4 Folklore Museum of Agios Nikolaos

MAP N4 ■ Konstantino Palaiologou 1 ■ 28410 25093 ■ Open May–Oct: 2–6:30pm daily

Overlooking Agios Nikolaos's harbour, the Folklore Museum houses colour-ful textiles and costumes, plus farming and fishing equipment.

## 5 Arolithos Museum of Agricultural History and Popular Art

MAP K4 ■ Arolithos village, 8 km/5 miles W of Heraklion on old highway ■ 2810 821050 ■ Open Apr–Oct: 9am–3pm; Nov–Mar: by appt ■ Adm ■ www.arolithos.com

This museum, linked with a holiday village, gives a taste of traditional Cretan life, with displays of art and household and agricultural items, plus a restaurant and bakery with wood-burning ovens.

## 6 War Museum of Askifou

MAP E4 ■ Askifou ■ 69778 27138 ■ 9am–9pm daily ■ Donations welcome ■ www.warmuseumaskifou.com

This museum was founded by George Hatzidakis, who wanted to collect every vestige of the Cretan struggle between 1941–44. Today, the collection has over 2,000 items.

**Memorabilia, War Museum of Askifou**

### 7 Cretan House Folklore Museum, Chania

MAP B6 ▪ 46B Chalidon ▪ 28210 90816 ▪ Summer: 9am–8pm (winter: to 5pm Mon–Sat) ▪ Adm (free for children)

Traditional looms and spinning wheels, richly coloured rugs, wall hangings and embroidery can be found at this delightful place.

### 8 Museum of Cretan Ethnology, Vori

MAP H5 ▪ Vori ▪ 28920 91110 ▪ Apr–Oct: 11am–5pm daily; closed winter except for groups by appt ▪ Adm ▪ www.cretanethnologymuseum.gr

Two floors of displays elucidate by-gone rural life with tools relating to everything from pig-butchering to boot-making and eel trapping.

**Vori's Museum of Cretan Ethnology**

### 9 Verekinthos Arts and Crafts Village

MAP D2 ▪ Souda ▪ Open 10am–2pm & 5:30–9pm Mon–Sat ▪ www.verekinthos.com

This formerly abandoned village near Souda port has been regenerated as an arts-and-crafts centre. With some 25 workshops hosting glassmakers, silversmiths, potters and weavers, it is a great place to shop for souvenirs.

### 10 Historical and Folklore Museum of Gavalochori

MAP E3 ▪ Gavalochori village ▪ 28250 23222 ▪ Open Apr–Oct: 9am–8pm Mon–Fri, 9am–7pm Sat, 10:30am–1:30pm & 5:30–8pm Sun; Nov–Mar: 8:30am–3pm daily ▪ Adm

This excellent small museum in an old Venetian-Ottoman mansion depicts the history and culture of the village.

---

## TOP 10 TRADITIONAL CRAFTS

**Embroidered tablecloths**

**1 Embroidery**
Rethymno was a major centre for embroidery, a skill introduced to Crete in the Byzantine era.

**2 Weaving**
Traditional hand looms are still in use, made from cypress, walnut or mulberry wood by skilled craftspeople.

**3 Spinning**
Older village women still spin wool into yarn using a spindle and distaff, a skill that hasn't changed since the time of the Minoans.

**4 Musical Instruments**
Crete has a very strong tradition of making musical instruments (see pp56–7), and many places still make the *lyra*, a three-stringed lap-fiddle, and the *laouto* (mandolin).

**5 Church Embroidery**
Crete's Orthodox monks and nuns embellish sumptuous church vestments with gold, silver and silk stitching.

**6 Wood Carving**
Olive, cypress and mulberry yield a hard wood much loved by skilled Cretan carpenters.

**7 Leatherwork**
Everything from shepherds' boots and mule harnesses to satchels, handbags and sheepskin garments.

**8 Silversmithing**
Silver jewellery and religious objects such as icon frames and crucifixes.

**9 Lace**
Silk *kopanelli* lace is made by bobbin weaving, a skill revived in Gavalochori.

**10 Antique Weapons**
The Cretan *pallikari* (warrior-hero) loved highly decorated weapons. Authentic antique weapons are highly valued.

#  Famous Cretans

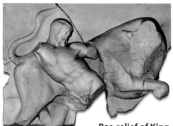

**Bas-relief of King Minos with the Minotaur**

## 1 King Minos

King of Crete, and both patron and tormentor of the ingenious Daedalus, Minos appears in the Greek myths as a tyrant. In fact, the legendary Minos is probably a composite of many Minoan kings.

## 2 Ioanna Angelopoulos-Daskalaki

Born in Heraklion in 1945, entrepreneur, politician and best-selling author Ioanna Angelopoulos-Daskalaki led Greece's winning bid to host the 2004 Summer Olympics. More recently, she chaired the committee for the bicentennial celebration of Greek independence in 2021.

## 3 George Psychoundakis

Born into a poor family in Rethymno, George served the resistance to the German occupation, both by acting as a guide to British forces and as a message-runner between groups, as told in Patrick Leigh Fermor's translation of Psychoundakis' memoir *The Cretan Runner*.

## 4 Michael Damaskinos

Artist Michael Damaskinos (c 1530–92) is the best-known of the Cretan School icon painters. His works are Byzantine in style but with Venetian influences. Some of his main pieces are in the Museum of Religious Art (*see p17*) in Heraklion.

## 5 El Greco

Born in the twilight years of Venetian rule in Crete, Domenikos Theotokopoulos (1541–1614) studied the icon painters of the Cretan School; their influence can be seen in the elongated features of his subjects and in his vivid use of colour. He trained under Titian in Italy, then moved to Spain, where he acquired his nickname, El Greco: "the Greek".

## 6 Vitsentzos Kornaros

Kornaros (1553–1613), a contemporary of El Greco and Damaskinos, was a leading figure in the Cretan renaissance and is remembered for his life's work, *Erotokritos*, Greece's greatest post-Byzantine work of epic literature. Sitia Airport bears his name.

**Effigy of Vitsentzos Kornaros**

## 7 Nikos Kazantzakis

Kazantzakis (1883–1957), born in Myrtia, near Heraklion, is best-known for his novel *Alexis Zorbas*, translated into English and filmed as *Zorba the Greek*. He was excommunicated by the Orthodox Church for his humanist views, and his self-penned epitaph reads: "I hope for nothing. I fear nothing. I am free."

**Grave of Nikos Kazantzakis**

**Greek premier Eleftherios Venizelos**

### 8 Eleftherios Venizelos

Born at Mournies, near Chania, Venizelos (1864–1936) made his reputation in the 1889 and 1897 uprisings. He led the campaign for union with Greece, and went on to become the Greek premier, dominating the nation's politics until the 1930s. Venizelos then became involved in a failed republican *coup d'etat* and was forced to flee the country, dying in exile in Paris.

### 9 Ioannis Daskalogiannis

Wealthy shipbuilder Ioannis Daskalogiannis (died 1771) raised the clans of the mountainous and inaccessible Sfakia region in the first major rebellion against the Ottomans in 1770. The uprising failed when Russian help did not materialize; Daskalogiannis surrendered at Frangokastello, from where he was taken to Heraklion to be tortured and skinned alive – not an uncommon penalty for rebels. Chania Airport was named after Daskalogiannis.

### 10 Chatzimichalis Dalianis

Dalianis, though a mainlander, ranks as an honorary Cretan for his local campaign during the Greek independence war. Ignoring local advice to wage guerrilla warfare like a Cretan, he and 385 followers chose in 1828 to occupy Frangokastello, where their enemies easily massacred them.

---

**TOP 10 WORKS OF ART AND LITERATURE**

**1 *Zorba the Greek* by Kazantzakis**
The freedom-loving spirit of Greece is to the fore in this tragi-comedy.

**2 *Erotokritos* by Vitsentzos Kornaros**
More than 10,000 lines of epic poetry written in the 15-syllable heptametric style, also sung as *mantinades* in Crete.

**3 Paintings by El Greco**
El Greco's only two paintings still in Crete are on display in Heraklion's Historical Museum *(see p17)*.

**4 Frescoes of Moni Varsamonero**
Later frescoes here, which span the period from 1360 to 1431, have been attributed to the 15th-century painter Konstantinos Rikos.

**5 Paintings by Lefteris Kanakakis**
Rethymno's Museum of Contemporary Art *(see p48)* houses a variety of this artist's works.

**6 *The Bull from the Sea* by Mary Renault**
A fictional retelling of the ancient myth of Theseus, Minos and the Minotaur.

**7 The Cretan Journal of Edward Lear**
Lear's illustrated diary of a journey to Crete in 1864.

**8 *The Island* by Victoria Hislop**
Set on Spinalonga and in Elounda, this novel tells the story of a young woman's discovery of her family's secret history.

**9 *Adoration of the Magi* by Michael Damaskinos**
A portrayal of the veneration of the infant Jesus (Museum of Religious Art, Heraklion).

**10 *Lord, Thou Art Great* by Ioannis Kornaros**
This is one of Crete's most dazzling, intricate and famous icons; it resides at Moni Toplou *(see p45)*.

**Kornaros's *Lord, Thou Art Great***

# 🔟 Myths and Legends

**Medieval artwork showing an episode from the story of Theseus and Ariadne**

### 1 Theseus and Ariadne

After defeating the Athenians in war, Minos demanded tribute of youths and maidens to give to the Minotaur. Theseus, prince of Athens, slew the Minotaur and escaped the labyrinth with the help of Minos's daughter Ariadne, who gave him a ball of thread to retrace his steps.

### 2 The Birth of Zeus

Zeus was the sixth child of the Titan Kronos, who had devoured his other children to prevent them from overthrowing him as he had overthrown his own father, Uranus, ruler of the old gods. Born in the Dikteon Cave in Crete, Zeus was hidden by his mother Rhea and raised in the Ideon Cave on Mount Ida. Zeus eventually poisoned Kronos, making him regurgitate his siblings, who overthrew the Titans to become the new gods and goddesses.

**Vase portraying the death of Talos**

### 3 Zeus and Europa

Though married to the goddess Hera, Zeus took many mortal lovers, one of whom was the princess Europa, daughter of the King of Phoenician Tyre. Taking the form of a white bull, Zeus carried Europa off to Crete, where he took her as his wife, siring three sons (including Minos).

### 4 The Immortal Plane Tree at Gortys

Zeus ravished Europa beneath this huge plane tree near the Roman ruins of Gortys. As a result, it is believed it never sheds its leaves, even in winter.

### 5 Talos the Bronze Giant

According to myth, Zeus created this bronze giant to defend Crete. Talos patrolled the coasts, hurling huge boulders to sink vessels that came too close. He was finally slain by Jason, with the aid of the sorceress Medea, who pointed out the giant's only weak spot, a vein near its ankle.

### 6 Nymphs of Dragolaki

The cave now known as the Dragolaki, or "Dragon's Lair", just outside the Sfakian mountain village of Agios Ioannis, is believed to be haunted by nereids, water-nymphs who were daughters of Nereus, a god of the sea.

###  Herakles and the Bull of Crete

The demigod Herakles, son of Zeus and the mortal woman Alcmene, was set 12 tasks by King Eurystheus, one of which was to capture and tame the untameable bull of Crete.

### 8 The Minotaur and the Labyrinth

In the myth of King Minos (one of the sons of Zeus and Europa), his queen Pasiphae bore a child, half bull and half man, after coupling with the sacred bull of Poseidon. Minos imprisoned this monster, the Minotaur, in a subterranean labyrinth.

### 9 The Drosoulites of Frangokastello

Every May, phantoms are said to emerge from nearby sand dunes and ride into the Frangokastello fortress (see p46). They are the ghosts of Chatzimichalis Dalianis (see p53) and his men, massacred by Muslim Cretans here in 1828.

### 10 Daedalus and Icarus

Daedalus and his son, Icarus, made wings of feathers held together with beeswax to escape imprisonment at the hands of King Minos – their punishment for helping Theseus slay the Minotaur. Icarus flew too high, and the sun melted the wax, causing him to plummet into the sea, but Daedalus reached safety in Sicily.

**Monument to Daedalus and Icarus, Agia Galini**

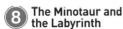

---

**TOP 10 CAVES**

**Inside the Dikteon Cave**

**1 Dikteon Cave (Dikteon Antron)**
Said to be the birthplace of Zeus, this cave above the Lasithi Plateau contains an artificial lake.

**2 Sfendoni**
The most spectacular cave on Crete is crammed with strange rock formations deep beneath the Idi range.

**3 Ideon Cave (Ideon Antron)**
This enormous cavern on the slopes of Mount Ida was the childhood hideout of Zeus.

**4 Kamares**
This cave on Mount Ida's southern face lends its name to the sophisticated Minoan pottery discovered here.

**5 Skotino**
This is one of Crete's largest caves. It was first dedicated to the local virgin goddess Britomartis and later became a sanctuary to Artemis.

**6 Inatos**
The goddess Ilithia, daughter of Zeus and Hera, was worshipped in this grotto, which delves into the sea-cliff above Tsoutsouros.

**7 Ilithia**
Archaic stone figures of pregnant women have been found in this cave, birthplace of the goddess Ilithia.

**8 Profitis Ilias**
As with Dikteon Cave, this cave near Arkalochori also claims to be the cradle of Zeus.

**9 Melidoni**
This cave was said to be the lair of Talos, the bronze giant created by Zeus.

**10 Cave of the Holy Fathers**
This gloomy cave in the remote Selino highlands is now a Greek Orthodox shrine.

# 🔟 Music and Instruments

**Traditional *askomandoura* player**

## 1 Askomandoura (Bagpipe)

The *askomandoura*, or Cretan bagpipe, was once a popular instrument around the southern Aegean islands. Like some other seldom heard instruments, it is undergoing a minor revival as a new wave of younger musicians rediscover their musical roots.

## 2 Voulgari

The *voulgari*, a Cretan version of the long-necked lute known in Turkey as the *saz*, was a popular solo instrument in Cretan town music but is rarely heard now.

## 3 Santouri

The hammer dulcimer, or *santouri*, is an import from Asia Minor into Greece, where it was not widely played until the 1920s. The *santouri* probably evolved from harp-like instruments, such as the *lyra* of the ancient Cretans.

## 4 Gerakokoudouna (Hawk Bells)

Cretan *lyra* players sometimes attach tiny copper or silver hawk bells to the horsehair bows with which the *lyra* is played. These little bells are not just ornamental; they provide an occasional lively and rhythmic jingling accompaniment.

## 5 Kithara (Guitar)

The guitar, whether acoustic or electric, has sadly ousted many of the older instruments and, even at village festivals, weddings and saints days, has become a standard member of the Cretan ensemble.

## 6 Lyra

The three-stringed *lyra* is typical of Crete, although it is also found on several nearby islands. Distinctly pear shaped, it has a rounded body and short, stout neck with no frets. The *lyra* player props the instrument on one knee and plays it with a small bow, producing melodies that may be merry, martial or melancholy.

**Musicians, including a *lyra* player**

### 7 Daoulaki, Toumbi

There are two names for this drum particular to villages around Sitia. The Daoulaki is played with two sticks, and varies in size from 12 inches (1 foot) to 48 inches (4 feet) in diameter. It is now rarely seen or heard.

### 8 Laouto

The *laouto* is the Cretan version of the mandolin and is one of the most important instruments for Cretan musicians and composers. It is usually used to provide a backing rhythm for the *lyra*, and like the *lyra* is an essential member of any Cretan ensemble. However, the *laouto* is increasingly heard as a solo instrument.

*Bouzoukis* and other instruments

### 9 Bouzouki

This long-necked, fretted lute with four double strings is of Middle Eastern origin but has existed in Greece since the 19th century. *Bouzouki* music gained popularity in mainland Greece after the exchange of Greek and Turkish populations in the 1920s, but until after World War II it was heard less in Crete.

### 10 Baglamas

Not indigenous to Crete, this small stringed instrument was made by prisoners or the poor from a dried gourd, or sometimes a tortoiseshell, for a sound box and wire strings.

---

**TOP 10 TRADITIONAL SONGS AND DANCES**

**Greek women dancing the *syrtos***

**1 Syrtos**
Performed all over Greece, the *syrtos* is undoubtedly the best-known of the Greek circle dances.

**2 Pidiktos**
The *pidiktos*, a dance from eastern Crete, involves great athletic leaps and bounds.

**3 Pentozalis**
The *pentozalis'* sprightly rhythms are reminiscent of the jigs and reels of Irish and Scottish folk music.

**4 Sousta**
A flirtatious couple's dance for the young, and a favourite at weddings and festivals.

**5 Hasapikos ("Zorba's Dance")**
The *hasapikos*, or "butcher's dance", provided inspiration for "Zorba's Dance" in the film *Zorba the Greek*.

**6 Siganos**
The dignified *siganos* dance is favoured by groups of men and women at festivals.

**7 Mandinades**
These traditional rhyming couplets, often satirical, are typical of Crete's rich oral tradition, with many improvised on the spot at festivals.

**8 Rizitika**
Stately elegies for historical events and personalities, with explicit or metaphorical lyrics, often performed as a capella, from Chania province.

**9 Haniotis**
The *haniotis* is a dignified line dance for men and women that originates from Chania.

**10 Tabachaniotika**
The Cretan, 1920s–30s version of the pan-Hellenic rembetika, songs of the urban underworld made popular by refugees from Asia Minor, some of whom settled in Chania.

# 🔟 Villages

**Shops lining the streets of Kritsa village**

## 1 Kritsa
MAP N5 ■ Lato: open 8:30am–3pm Tue–Sun

Sweeping views downhill and a reputation as one of the best craft centres of eastern Crete ensures that Kritsa sees its fair share of tourism. Its main street is packed with shops selling leather satchels and sandals, embroidery and brightly patterned rugs. About an hour's walk from Kritsa is the minor archaeological site of Lato, where you can see the remains of a Classical Greek city.

## 2 Argyroupoli
MAP E4

Western Crete's prettiest mountain village is tucked in the foothills of the Lefka Ori, on the site of the Hellenistic town of Lappa. The slopes of its valley setting flourish with lush greenery, watered by natural springs. Argyroupoli makes a good base for fairly easy walking in the surrounding hills.

## 3 Elos
MAP B3

Elos is one of the settlements known as the Enea Choria ("Nine Villages"), which are set among the chestnut forests of the Selino region. At 600 m (1,970 ft) above sea level, it can be pleasantly cool in summer. Elos has a 14th-century Byzantine chapel and a ruined Ottoman aqueduct.

## 4 Alikianos
MAP C2

A ruined Venetian castle *(see p46)* of the aristocratic Molini family and a noted 14th-century church of Agios Ioannis (or "Ai-Kir Yanni" in local Cretan dialect) are the prime sights of Alikianos. The village is picturesque in itself, however, and is surrounded by citrus groves.

## 5 Kournas
MAP E3

Kournas nestles at the foot of Mount Dafnomadara, close to Crete's only freshwater lake. Its old stone houses cluster around a steep main street, and the village has two Byzantine-Venetian churches, dedicated to Agios Georgios and Agia Eirini.

### 6 Hamezi
**MAP Q5**

Above the Bay of Sitia, Hamezi has been inhabited since the Minoan era. Remnants of Minoan buildings can be seen on a hilltop from the present village, which is a peaceful cluster of stone cottages, offset by colourful displays of flowers.

### 7 Ethia
**MAP Q5**

During Venetian occupation, this now desolate hamlet was the fief of the De Mezzo family. Their family manor has been admirably restored and has a small display on life in Venetian Crete.

### 8 Topolia
**MAP B3**

This village, en route from Kastelli to Paleochora, stands amid farm terraces, fields and olive groves, in a well watered valley which leads into Topolia Gorge. Its small church of Agia Paraskevi dates from the late Byzantine era.

**Stone church in the village of Axos**

### 9 Axos
**MAP H4**

On the most direct route from Perama to Anogeia, off the old highway between Heraklion and Perama, Axos has striking views and an attractive Byzantine church dedicated to Agia Eirini. The village is a popular stop for excursion groups, and its tavernas become busy around lunchtime. On the hillside above Axos are a few scattered remnants of an ancient settlement.

### 10 Voila
**MAP Q5**

Voila is Crete's most dramatic ghost village, with lizards scuttling across its ruined walls and crumbling doorways. Voila is overlooked by the tumbledown walls of a Venetian hilltop castle and an Ottoman tower, and the only building still intact is the church of Agios Georgios. Surprisingly, two Ottoman-era drinking fountains still provide visitors with fresh water.

**Aerial view of Lake Kournas**

# 🔟 Beach Resorts

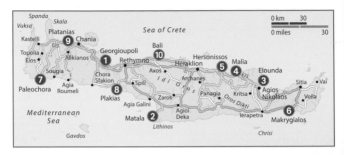

## 1️⃣ Georgioupoli
**MAP E3**

At the mouth of the Perastikos River,, 20 km (12 miles) west of Rethymno, lies the quiet resort of Georgioupoli. The hub of the village is provided by a taverna-lined square shaded by eucalyptus trees. Georgioupoli's hotels and self-catering accommodation is spread out along a vast sandy beach.

## 2️⃣ Matala
**MAP G6**

Matala's coves of coarse sand mixed with pebbles, surrounded by rocky red cliffs harbouring Roman cave-tombs, made the place a magnet for hippy travellers in the 1960s. Its tourism is more orthodox now, but Matala is still pleasantly low-key. A good base for exploring Gortys and Phaistos.

**Artificial caves at Matala beach**

**Crystal-clear waters at Elounda**

## 3️⃣ Elounda
**MAP N4**

Overlooking the turquoise waters of the Gulf of Mirabello and Spinalonga island, Elounda lies 11 km (7 miles) north of Agios Nikolaos, in eastern Crete. Formerly a peaceful fishing village, it is now one of Greece's most luxurious destinations, with the highest concentration of five-star resort hotels after Santorini.

## 4️⃣ Malia
**MAP M4**

With its great sandy beach and close proximity to Heraklion International Airport, Malia was destined to become one of the island's liveliest package holiday resorts. In July and August it is thronged, attracting a young crowd with its watersports and pulsing nightlife. There are peaceful spots to be found, too.

###  Hersonissos
MAP M4

The biggest and busiest of the island's resorts, Hersonissos straddles the north coast highway – a long double strip of hotels, bars, restaurants, dance clubs and shops. Catering mainly for package holiday-makers, it has now almost merged with the neighbouring resorts of Stalida and Malia.

Sheltered Souda beach, just west of Plakias

###  Makrygialos
MAP Q5

Makrygialos has a great beach in southeastern Crete, a swathe of grey sand and shingle beneath pine-covered slopes. This and its neighbour Analipsi have melded into a single chain of tavernas and guesthouses.

### Paleochora
MAP B4

On a headland crowned by a dilapidated Venetian castle, Paleochora is part-fishing village, part-resort. It has a crescent of yellow sand on the west side of the promontory and a less crowded pebbly beach on the east.

###  Plakias
MAP F4

A huge sweep of clean grey sand attracts visitors to this small south-coast resort, but there are even better nearby beaches just west at Souda (backed by palm trees) and east around Damnoni, where there are three coves to choose from. Plakias is one of the island's quieter beach resorts, and its accommodation is mostly self-catering apartments.

###  Platanias
MAP C2

The beach at Platanias stretches for 2 km (1 mile) west of Chania's Old Town and is backed by a strip of hotels, cafés and souvenir shops. Given its close location to Chania, Platanias is a lively hub on Crete's northwest coast.

###  Bali
MAP H3

A small resort, purpose built around coves on the north coast, Bali comes to life in high season, when its "Paradise Beach" (officially Livadi) glistens with sunbathing bodies.

**Holiday-makers on the beach at Bali**

# 🔟 Areas of Natural Beauty

## ① Imbros Gorge
**MAP D4** ■ **Open 7am–sunset**
■ **Adm charge in summer**

The Imbros Gorge extends between the villages of Komitades and Imbros. Its narrowest point is 2 m (6 ft) wide. It takes 3 hours to walk through it.

**Imbros Gorge's dramatic landscape**

## ② White Mountains (Lefka Ori)
**MAP C–D4**

The White Mountain region of Crete is one of Europe's pockets of wilderness, a region of savage, gaunt mountains traversed by deep gorges through which small streams flow in springtime. The best-known of these is the lovely Samaria Gorge *(see pp30–31)*. In winter, the White Mountain peaks are covered with snow, but in summer temperatures can rise to more than 35° C (95° F).

## ③ Lake Votamos (Zaros)
**MAP J5**

Fed by an underground spring which provides eastern Crete with most of its bottled mineral water, Lake Votamos is a deep-blue ring of cool, clear water surrounded by flinty, barren slopes. Tavernas near the shore serve grilled trout from the lake, and a good gorge walk starts nearby.

## ④ Aspros Potamos
**MAP P5**

The valley of the "white river" – which, like most Cretan watercourses, flows only in winter and spring – reaches the sea at the eastern end of Makrygialos beach. Surrounded by boulder-covered slopes, pines, terraced fields and olive groves, Aspros Potamos offers a pleasant walk with handsome Pefki village as the ideal start-point.

## ⑤ Omalos Plateau
**MAP C3**

A fertile plain ringed by rocky slopes, the plateau lies 1,050 m (3,445 ft) up on the northern side of the White Mountains. Millennia of winter rains have washed the topsoil down from the surrounding slopes to create this upland oasis. Most people tend to pass through without stopping, but, especially during spring, this is one of the prettiest, most peaceful spots in Crete.

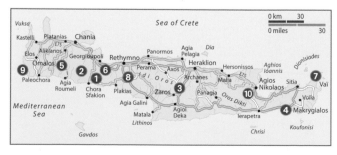

**Ruins on the islet of Elafonisi**

### (6) Lake Kournas
**MAP E3**

Terrapins and migrating water birds are among the wildlife to be spotted in and around Crete's main body of fresh water. The lake is prettiest in spring and early summer and is ideal for renting a boat.

**Birds on the shores of Lake Kournas**

### (7) Vaï
**MAP R4**

A group of sturdy native Cretan palms on a crescent of beach at Vaï is the largest of several such around Crete; others include Preveli and Souda, Plakias. The species *Phoenix theophrasti* is named after the botanist who discovered it.

### (8) Kourtaliotiko Gorge
**MAP F4**

Frogs, terrapins, crabs and tiny water snakes splash and slither in freshwater pools at the bottom of the pretty canyon which emerges below Preveli on the south coast.

### (9) Elafonisi
**MAP A4**

This tiny islet, a stone's throw from the mainland, may in the past have been a preserve for deer since its name means "deer island". Between Elafonisi *(see p84)* and the shore is a lagoon of turquoise water. It is possible to reach the island simply by wading.

### (10) Lasithi
**MAP M4**

Few of the thousands of white-sailed buildings in this "Plain of Windmills" still exist in working order. That said, the drive to this bowl of rich farm-land surrounded by mountains is stunning in itself. Lasithi's patch-work of fertile fields, gardens and orchards strikes a contrast with the treeless grey slopes surrounding it.

**Windmill on the Lasithi Plateau**

# TOP 10 Mountain Walks

**Hiking through the Samaria Gorge**

White Mountains is spectacular, but only for very fit, experienced mountain walkers. The White Mountains rise to a 2,453 m (8,048 ft) peak, and walkers should note that it is bitterly cold in winter and scorchingly hot in summer.

## 3 Imbros Gorge
MAP D4

The gorge, which cuts through the eastern foothills of the White Mountains, is a slightly shorter hike than the better-known and much busier Samaria Gorge, but it is almost as spectacular and – especially in spring and autumn – allows you to escape from the crowds of day visitors.

## 4 Hochlakies Gorge
MAP R4

Beginning just outside Hochlakies village near Sitia, an easy, distinct path threads this gorge past striking rock formations. At the bottom, 45 minutes along, lies idyllic, sandy Karoumes beach. After a swim, walkers can retrace their steps.

## 1 Samaria Gorge

Passing through the rugged scenery of the Samaria National Park, the Samaria Gorge is Crete's most popular walk. The track descends steeply at first from the Omalos plateau, then passes through pine woods, wildflower meadows and ruined villages to emerge at the small resort of Agia Roumeli (see pp30–31).

## 2 Across the Lefka Ori
MAP C4–D4 ■ Eos Mountain Refuge, Kallergi ■ 28210 44647 ■ Open Apr–Oct

A two-day traverse of the savage, treeless wilderness of the high

## 5 Climbing Mount Ida
MAP H4

The ascent of 2,456 m (8,060 ft) Mount Ida, Crete's highest mountain, begins on the Nida Plateau. The trail (7–8 hours up and down) is best tackled on a long May or June day; expect snowdrifts near the summit chapel.

**Trekking across the Lefka Ori**

**Kapetaniana, near Mount Kofinas**

### ⑥ Mount Kofinas
**MAP K6**

Give yourself half a day to climb from the remote village of Kapetaniana to the summit of Mount Kofinas, 1,231 m (4,040 ft) and back. There are fine views of Mount Ida, the Dikti range and the south coast.

### ⑦ Sougia–Agia Roumeli
**MAP C4**

This eight-hour trek begins in the beach resort of Sougia, on the southwestern fringe of the White Mountains, and climbs first through fields and pastureland, then meadows of wild-flowers and pine woods, onto barren slopes high above the sea, before descending to Agia Roumeli. It is a difficult trek requiring astute navigational skills and a good map.

### ⑧ E4 European Long-Distance Path

Recommended only for very fit and experienced walkers, this is a long, arduous trek with variable route markings: yellow-and-black metal signs, poles or painted rocks. It is, effectively, a traverse of the entire island of Crete that takes at least 30 days to complete, from Kissamos in the west to Palaikastro in the east.

### ⑨ Zakros Gorge
**MAP R5**

The walk through the Zakros Gorge, also known as the "Valley of the Dead", snakes through a dramatic landscape, following a dry stream bed through eroded limestone cliffs with caves that were used as tombs by the Minoans. An aqueduct supplies potable water.

### ⑩ Agia Roumeli–Loutro
**MAP C4–D4**

This four-hour walk follows a path along the sand and pebble beach of Agios Pavlos, then climbs the steep Sellouda cobbled stair-path onto a high, pine-wooded plateau. It later descends into the Aradena Gorge, before zigzagging down a steep cliff to the delightful holiday village of Loutro.

**The coastal village of Loutro**

# 🔟 Wildlife

**A Cretan spiny mouse with her young**

## 1 Cretan Spiny Mouse

The Cretan spiny mouse is unique to the island. Like most small rodents, it is nocturnal and is therefore not the easiest of the island's mammals to see. Look out for its endearingly large ears and blunt spines against rocky slopes at twilight.

## 2 Scops Owl

The tiny scops owl, with its grey plumage and bright yellow eyes, is common in Crete. This bird nests in holes in battered stone walls and roosts on roadside telephone poles or tree stumps. You are most likely to see scops owls at dusk, but after dark they can often be heard calling to each other – a monotonous, one-note hoot.

## 3 Scarce Swallowtail

Europe's largest butterfly is the dramatically patterned scarce swallowtail, its pale-yellow or white wings marked with dark zebra stripes and red and blue eye-spots. A strong flyer, this butterfly may be seen all over Crete in summer.

**Scarce swallowtail**

## 4 Gecko

Big-eyed gecko lizards, with sucker-tipped fingers that enable them to cling to walls and ceilings, inhabit many buildings, especially tourist lodgings around the island, coming out after dark to hunt insects. You may see several clinging to the wall near outdoor lamps, waiting to snap up moths and mosquitoes attracted by the light.

## 5 Lammergeier

The rare lammergeier vulture, Europe's largest bird of prey, may be seen soaring above the Omalos Plateau or in the high reaches of the White Mountains. Nicknamed the "bone-breaker", the lammergeier feeds on the carcasses of goats and sheep, and sometimes smashes bones open by dropping them from a great height to reach the marrow.

**The majestic lammergeier vulture**

## 6 Cretan Wild Cat

Cretan shepherds have long been claiming that the wilder parts of Mount Ida are home to a large wild cat known locally as the *fourogattos*. The first live specimen of this elusive beast was caught in the mid-1990s by Italian zoologists. Weighing 5.5 kg (12 lbs), with a tawny pelt and a formidable snarl, the Cretan wild cat is a rather startling re-discovery.

### 7 Pelican

The Dalmatian pelican, which breeds in the lakes and wetlands of northern Greece, Macedonia and Albania, migrates south to the Nile Delta for the winter. A few birds sometimes make landfall in Crete after being blown off course by storms, or by becoming exhausted by the force of strong headwinds.

**Dalmatian pelican mid-flight**

### 8 Cretan Argus Butterfly

This beautiful dark-brown butterfly is limited to the higher slopes of the Dikti range and Ida mountain. It is increasingly endangered through loss of habitat.

### 9 Eleonora's Falcon

The very rare Eleonora's falcon breeds on some of Crete's offshore islands and can sometimes be seen performing its remarkable aerobatics above the steep cliffs of Zakros in eastern Crete.

### 10 Cretan Wild Goat

The Cretan wild goat, locally called *agrimi* or *kri-kri*, is one of Europe's rarest mammals. Perhaps 2,000 of these shy creatures live in the Samaria Gorge National Park, on the cliffs of the White Mountains and on Dia Islet off Crete's north coast.

**A male Cretan wild goat**

---

**TOP 10 TREES AND FLOWERS**

**Cretan ebony on a mountainside**

**1 Cretan Ebony**
Putting out spikes of pink flowers in spring, the Cretan ebony clings to steep, rocky cliffs and mountainsides.

**2 Juniper**
Two species of this plant thrive on Crete – one stabilising sand dunes as salt-tolerant shrubs, the other inland as massive trees.

**3 Dragon Arum**
With its foul-smelling red flower and spike, the dragon arum is a motif in several Minoan frescoes and a reality in shady spots beneath trees.

**4 Yellow Bee Orchid**
The yellow bee orchid, bearing flowers that imitate the insects it attracts, blooms on mountain slopes in spring.

**5 Catchfly**
With its ragged bright-pink flowers, the catchfly traps insects on the sap-coated hairs of its sticky stems.

**6 Yellow Horned Poppy**
This poppy lends a splash of colour to rocky stretches of the Cretan foreshore.

**7 Giant Reed**
The giant calamus reed grows as high as 4 m (13 ft) on the banks of streams.

**8 Autumn Cyclamen**
In October, flowering from apparently barren ground, the pink autumn cyclamen signals the end of summer.

**9 Spring Crocus**
This mauve flower with vivid yellow stamens flowers early in the year.

**10 Evergreen Plane**
Endemic to Crete, the tough evergreen plane has evolved to cope with the harsh environment. It is a subspecies of the common Oriental plane.

# 🔟 Nightlife

**Dining al fresco in Paleochora**

## 1 Paleochora
MAP B4

A hippy hideout well into the 1980s, Paleochora (see p102) is still a laid-back spot. A handful of relaxed music bars are scattered along the Chalikia Beach (east of Paleochora town), and there are a couple of open-air clubs just outside the town.

## 2 Agios Nikolaos
MAP N4

Agios Nikolaos (see pp112–13) has a surprisingly lively after-dark scene compared with its day-time placidity. The town's nightlife hot spot is the pedestrianized Odos 25 Martiou (running uphill from the southwestern corner of the harbour), where there are half a dozen music bars, with as many again around the harbour. The town's club scene is more limited, with only one or two lively clubs.

## 3 Agia Pelagia
MAP K3

Lying 20 km (12 miles) west of Heraklion, this low-key resort is built into a steep hillside overlooking a sheltered bay, rimmed by a curving sandy beach. In summer, it is a popular after-dark escape for locals, who come here for the waterside cocktail bars and seafood tavernas.

## 4 Platanias
MAP C2

Platanias (see p105) is where most of Chania's younger residents go to party during summer weekends. There are at least a dozen great clubs, most with open-air dance floors. These clubs do not really start to get lively until well after midnight.

## 5 Agia Galini
MAP G5

This small resort (see p93) has made catering to the party crowd its speciality. The cluster of bars and dance clubs around the harbour are buzzing by 11pm, allowing you to club-hop until the early hours.

**The harbour of Agios Nikolaos at twilight**

**Busy taverna in Hersonissos**

### 6 Hersonissos
MAP M4

A former fishing village, Hersonissos (see p93) has become a continuous strip of bars, clubs, restaurants and guesthouses, stretching along some of the north coast's better beaches. Expect a multilingual clientele.

### 7 Rethymno
MAP F3

Most of the liveliest music-bars line Rethymno's (see pp26–7) old-town lanes inland from the harbour. Later on, the nightlife scene shifts to the open-air clubs in the resort area, along the seafront east of the centre.

### 8 Ierapetra
MAP N6

The only city on the southern coast, Ierapetra comes alive at night, with music bars, pubs, fish taverns and restaurants opening their doors along the seaside promenade. Music events take things up a notch in the summer.

### 9 Heraklion
MAP K3

The nightlife scene in Crete's capital (see pp16–17) is more staid than in the resorts. Young locals congregate in the cafés and music bars located around Plateia Venizelou and Odos Chandakou.

### 10 Chania
MAP D2

Music blasts out from most of the cafés and bars along the harbourfront in Chania (see pp20–21) in the summer, and if you prefer an evening of bar-hopping and café-crawling to a night in the dance clubs, there are few better places in Crete. After midnight, younger Chaniots head to the clubs of Koum Kapi (east of the old walls) or Platanias (see p105).

**Tavernas in the old town of Chania**

# 🔟 Food and Drink

**Classic *patsas* soup, made with tripe**

## 1 Soup (Kreatosoupa and Patsas)

Cretan cooking makes full use of all cuts of meat. *Kreatosoupa* (meat soup) is made from the bones and left-over scraps of goat, mutton or beef, while *patsas* is a rich soup made with tripe. At festivals, a goat is traditionally slaughtered and spit-roasted for the guests.

## 2 Tsikoudia

Similar to Italian grappa, *Tsikoudia* or *raki* is a colourless spirit distilled from the skins and stems left after grape pressing. You may see market traders starting the day with a shot of *tsikoudia* and a strong coffee. It is also drunk after meals.

**_Tsikoudia_, a traditional Cretan spirit**

## 3 Cheeses (Staka and Myzithra)

Far more delicious than the ubiquitous feta are Crete's own cheeses. These delicious products include *myzithra*, which is made from fresh sheep's milk, and *piktogalo*, a thick white cheese made in Chania.

## 4 Beer

Crete has a few microbreweries that are well worth trying. Cretan in Chania makes three Charma labels (dunkel, lager and pale ale), while Brink's of Rethymno province is known for its organic dark and light beers.

## 5 Wines

Cretan wines are becoming more sophisticated as makers introduce techniques pioneered by global producers. Most great wineries are in the Peza area of the Heraklion region, but there are also some good wineries that can be visited near Sitia and Chania.

## 6 Cretan Sausages (Loukanika)

*Loukanika* – small spicy pork sausages – are found all over Greece, but those from Crete are reckoned to be among the best. The most famous ones hail from Sfakia district, and are served preferably grilled, though sometimes fried. They are a staple of *meze-dopoleia* (titbit food joints).

## 7 Greek Coffee (Kafes Ellinikos)

Finely ground robusta coffee beans and sugar are boiled together in small metal pots to make a thick, black drink, which is served up to customers in a tiny cup along with a tall glass of water. To order a sweet coffee, ask for *glyko*; *metrio* is for medium-sweet; and for coffee without any sugar, order *sketo*.

**Selection of fresh olives for sale**

### ⑧ Olives

Crete and olives are basically inseparable. The olive has provided not only food, but also oil for lamps, and wood for fuel – without it, Crete might not have become the cradle of Minoan civilization. Olives are sold in a bewildering array of sizes and flavours, and Cretan olive oil (especially from Kolymvari area) is well-known overseas for its quality.

**Snails with tomato sauce**

### ⑨ Snails (Chochlioi)

Once a valuable source of protein, snails are now regarded as a delicacy. *Chochlioi* are either stewed in red sauce or sautéed *bourbouristi*-style with garlic, herbs and olive oil. Waiters give free extraction lessons.

### ⑩ Stamnagathi (Spiny Chicory)

Spiny chicory is the most esteemed of Crete's many wild greens, served lightly blanched. The picking season is early autumn, but popularity ensures that it is grown throughout the year.

## TOP 10 CRETAN HERBS

### 1 Dittany
Taking its name from the Dikti mountains, this variety of oregano is unique to Crete and has long been credited with restorative powers.

### 2 Sage
Sage from the Cretan mountains is a favourite medicinal *tisane*, and is said to cure fever and sore throats.

### 3 Saffron
Deriving from the crocus flower, costly saffron is used sparingly to add colour and flavour to soups and stews.

### 4 Fennel
Growing profusely in the countryside, this member of the carrot family has both edible shoots – ideal for stuffing fish – and a root used for cooking, particularly with cuttlefish.

### 5 Malotira
Endemic to Crete, this plant is thought to have healing properties, and is often consumed as Malotira tea.

### 6 Cinnamon
Cretans acquired a taste for spices during the Ottoman and Venetian eras. Today, cinnamon flavours desserts like *ryzokalo* (rice pudding) and sweet pies.

### 7 Oregano
This herb is a defining flavour in many Greek dishes, from fish to meat.

### 8 Rosemary
Growing in abundance, rosemary is used by Cretans mainly to flavour fish dishes.

### 9 Mint
This ubiquitous wild herb scents the air on rural walks and flavours dozens of local dishes such as *keftedes* (meatballs).

### 10 Thyme
Sweet-scented thyme, with its deep purple flowers, grows wild on Crete's roadsides and hillsides.

**A thyme bush in full bloom**

# TOP10 Restaurants

**The picturesque courtyard of Rethymno's Avli restaurant**

**1 Avli, Rethymno**

This elegant courtyard restaurant *(see p109)* is one of the best in Rethymno. Traditional grilled and roasted meat dishes are served alongside Cretan favourites such as *apatzia* (smoked sausages) and roast goat.

**2 Tamam, Chania**

Popular with Chania's locals as well as with holiday-makers, Tamam *(see p109)* has a menu that takes in cuisines from around the shores of the Eastern Mediterranean. Good choices for vegetarians, too.

**Outdoor tables at Tamam, Chania**

**3 Prima Plora, Rethymno**

In a dreamy seaside location facing Rethymno's Fortezza, this Mediterranean restaurant and wine bar *(see p109)* serves local favourites, from ceviche to tuna tartare. The wine is excellent.

**4 The Balcony, Sitia**

Run by a Cretan-French couple, Balcony *(see p119)* offers Greek fusion cooking with Mexican, Asian and French influences. Wild herbs and local produce are extensively used in dishes ranging from traditional Cretan snails with tomato and goat's cheese to pork fillet with yogurt and pilaf rice.

**5 The Five Restaurant, Chania**

This beautiful waterfront restaurant *(see p109)* in Nea Chora serves Cretan favourites alongside local wines and beers.

**6 Methexis, Paleochora**

On the east waterfront away from the main restaurant district, Methexis *(see p109)* excels at keenly priced creative Cretan recipes cooked in limited quantities. Try to arrive early to sit at a prime table. It is open all year round.

### 7 Thalasses, Heraklion

Located east of the city centre in Nea Alikarnassos, close to the airport, 7 Thalasses (which means "seven seas") is regarded by locals as one of Crete's best fish restaurants (see p97). Delights include squid with pesto, and sea bass with truffles and asparagus, plus a selection of exquisite sushi.

### 8 Poulis, Elounda

In a beautiful location on the waterfront, Poulis (see p119) even has tables on a floating pontoon which, when lit up at night, make you feel like you are dining on a yacht. The fish, octopus and calamari are excellent, and the traditional meze are exceptional.

### 9 Veneto, Rethymno

The 14th-century vaults that house Veneto (see p109) once contained a refectory for monks living in the cells above. Guests can sample the tasting menu as well as the chef's take on traditional local recipes at the pretty courtyard restaurant. Veneto's menu features a number of Cretan specialities, and the service is excellent.

**Veneto restaurant's historic setting**

### 10 The Ferryman, Elounda

With tables by the water's edge, this spot (see p119) was named after the BBC serial *Who Pays the Ferryman*, which was filmed here. It serves Cretan specialities such as fresh lobster and roast mountain goat.

---

**TOP 10 FISH SERVED IN CRETAN RESTAURANTS**

**Pan-fried *barbounia*, or red mullet**

**1 Barbounia**
Small red mullet appear on almost every tourist menu, pan-fried or grilled. Each fish provides only a few delicious mouthfuls – beware of bones!

**2 Melanouria**
Saddled bream, common in spring, is variably sized, tasty and usually grilled.

**3 Fangri**
Red porgy, prized for its delicate white flesh, is grilled and served whole; usually (but not always) one of the most expensive fish on the menu.

**4 Marides**
Tiny picarel are dipped in flour and shallow-fried, then served with shredded lettuce and a slice of lemon.

**5 Lavraki**
Sea bass is baked in olive oil, red wine vinegar and rosemary, served whole.

**6 Sardeles**
Sardines are wrapped in vine leaves to seal in flavour and moisture, then grilled. Salted and pickled sardines are often served as meze.

**7 Xifias**
Swordfish keeps its flavour well when frozen, so it is a favourite with restaurateurs.

**8 Skorpina**
The evil-looking scorpion fish is surprisingly tasty and essential in Cretan fish soup; also served grilled.

**9 Tonnos**
Tuna steaks are best savoured in spring and autumn, when tuna migrate through Cretan waters.

**10 Gopes**
These nondescript, bony little fish are the cheapest on the menu, but delicious once the bones are removed.

# TOP 10 Rural Tavernas

**Colourful plate of typical Cretan food**

## 1 Piperia, Pefki

Piperia *(see p119)* serves traditional Cretan dishes prepared from seasonal and locally-sourced ingredients. Visitors can enjoy delicious food along with spectacular views of the rugged southern coast and a relaxed atmosphere. On weekend nights, there may be live music and dancing.

## 2 Taverna Plateia, Myrthios

This village taverna *(see p109)* attracts crowds for the views from its terrace over the Libyan Sea. Half of Crete seems to turn up on Sundays, but it is quieter during the week, with more time to enjoy the traditional cuisine and soak up the relaxing ambience.

## 3 Ta Douliana, Douliana

Situated in the centre of the tiny village of Douliana, this typical taverna's rickety wooden tables and chairs are set on a pretty terrace shaded by vines *(see p109)*. The menu focuses on traditional, hearty fare such as *arni avgolemono* (lamb with lemon sauce). The main dishes are complemented with a good selection of local cheeses and wines. There's a roaring log fire for cooler evenings.

## 4 Goules, Goulediana

MAP F4 ■ 10 km (6 miles) south of Rethymno ■ 28310 41001 ■ €

This traditional village taverna offers Cretan food with a twist. A highlight of the menu here is the roast pork in wine and honey sauce.

## 5 Taverna Arxaia Lappa, Argyroupoli

In Argyroupoli, known for its natural springs and cascades, this taverna *(see p109)* serves traditional lamb *lemonato* (roasted lamb with lemon and potatoes), chicken and pork dishes, as well as generous portions of salads. The delicious dishes are heightened by the friendly service.

## 6 Tou Zisis, Misiria

Zisis looks rather simple and un-prepossessing at first, housed in a drab concrete building. However inside, it *(see p109)* serves some of the best food around – the grilled lamb alone is worth the short trip east of Rethymno.

## 7 El Greco, Lendas

El Greco *(see p97)* has the day's dishes displayed in the kitchen for diners to choose from. Also on the menu are fish, octopus and grilled meats, served on a series of terraces above the beach. Book ahead.

**Dining on the terrace at El Greco**

### ⑧ Taverna Androulidakis, Gonia

**MAP F3** ▪ 6974 006027 ▪ €

Visit this family-run taverna for atmospheric alfresco summer dining. The extensive menu of Cretan favourites features dishes prepared with home-grown produce.

### ⑨ Kalliotzina, Koutsouras

An old-fashioned taverna *(see p119)* with seaside tables, where visitors can venture into the kitchen to choose from the traditional dishes of the day or to watch a fish being grilled. Enjoy live Greek music twice a week.

**Table with sea views at Kalliotzina**

### ⑩ Mourelo Cretan Cuisine, Ammoudara

With a bright decor and outdoor seating, this restaurant *(see p97)* serves excellent steaks, generous salads, seafood and refreshing cocktails.

---

**TOP 10 WINES AND WINERIES**

**Wine cellar with various offerings**

**1 Domaine Fantaxometocho**
Owned by Boutari, this Skalani village winery produces an excellent red from Kotsifali and Mandilaria grapes.

**2 Domaine Paterianakis**
This micro-winery makes an excellent rosé from Kotsifali and Syrah grapes.

**3 Lyrarakis Winery**
This 1966 winery has rescued near-extinct, local varieties by combining Vilana, Vidiano and Muscat Spina grapes.

**4 Miliarakis Metikos**
A rich, heavy red made from syrah and cabernet sauvignon grapes, best drunk with red meats and heavy sauces.

**5 Sitia Cooperative Sitia White**
A crisp, dry wine from blended Vilana and Thrapsathiri grapes, ideal for pairing with the local seafood.

**6 Klados White Diva**
Complex and fruity with the herbal aroma of Crete's most valued grape, Vidiano, this wine has a balanced acidity.

**7 Economou Liatiko**
Produced from vineyards on the very remote Ziros plateau in Crete's far southeast, this complex red shows a native grape at its best.

**8 Miliarakis Estate PDP Red**
One of the oldest Peza-region wineries produces this rich, oak-aged red from Kotsifali and Mandilaria grapes.

**9 Gavalas An Rosé**
Gavalas Winery prides itself on its organic production methods; this crisp rosé combines native Kotsifali with imported Cabernet Sauvignon grapes.

**10 Lyrarakis Malvasia**
Known in England as Malmsey, this dessert wine was exported everywhere by the Venetians. It is revived now in this blend of four white grapes, sun dried and oak-aged for a year.

# 🔟 Cafés and Mezedopoleia

**Dining on meze at Ouzeri tou Terzaki, in the heart of Heraklion Old Town**

## ① Avli tou Devkaliona, Heraklion

**MAP S1** ■ Lysimáhou Kalokerinoú ■ 28102 44215

A night-time evergreen, right behind the Historical Museum, with courtyard seating beside a dry Venetian wall-fountain. Tuck into classic *raki* pairings such as *volvoi* (pickled hyacinth bulbs) or delicate *keftedakia* (mini-meatballs).

## ② Koukouvayia, Chania

**MAP D2** ■ Tafoi Venizelon

On a hillside close to the Venizelos family tombs, this café is much loved by locals for its homemade desserts – try the *zoumero,* a fluffy chocolate cake dipped in rich, warm chocolate syrup.

## ③ Avli, Agios Nikolaos

**MAP N4** ■ P Georgiou 12 ■ 28410 82479

This garden *mezedopoleio* is set in a courtyard shaded by grapevines and lemon trees. Delicious *mezedes,* as well as more elaborate dishes, are served with house wine made from their own vineyards in the Sitia hills.

## ④ Ouzeri tou Terzaki, Heraklion

A favourite among locals, Terzaki *(see p96)* is one of a row of *mezedopoleia* on this narrow alley in the heart of the city. There are substantial meals on the menu including mussels *saganaki,* seafood, as well as pasta and risotto; however, a drink and a selection of *mezedes* (such as the cheese-stuffed artichoke) is particularly recommended.

## ⑤ Kaaren's, Elounda

Check out this café's *(see p118)* delicious breakfast, brunch, lunch and early evening cocktails for a welcome change from the regular taverna fare.

## ⑥ Kirkor, Heraklion

A classic bakery-café right by the Morosini fountain, Kirkor *(see p96)* has tables spreading out into the square. The speciality is *bougatsa,* a flaky pastry available in either sweet-cream or salty-cheese versions. Offering a variety

**Cheese pie, typical of Kirkor's menu**

of coffees, it makes a perfect spot for breakfast, and it opens very early.

### 7 Agios Bar, Paleochora

This café-bar *(see p108)* has been a local institution for more than 100 years. It is known for cocktails crafted from local *raki*, brandy and its own artisan coffee blends.

### 8 The Bitters Bar, Heraklion
**MAP T2 ■ Platia Venizelou**

A favourite with locals, this speakeasy style bar offers a range of imaginative cocktails that can be enjoyed through the night. The bar is also open in the morning for coffee.

### 9 New York Beach Club, Hersonissos

Overlooking the bay, this beach bar *(see p96)*, with its relaxed setting and wide array of drinks and snacks, is a good party spot.

**Diners at Ta Halkina**

### 10 Ta Halkina, Chania
**MAP B5 ■ Akti Tombazi 29-30**

This is one of the few old-port restaurants favoured by locals. The highlight of Ta Halkina is the excellent Cretan cuisine and the live acoustic music played on most nights. The option of outdoor tables is available for those who find the music too loud.

## TOP 10 MEZEDES DISHES

**A plate of shrimp *saganaki***

**1 Saganaki**
Either a slab of fried or grilled cheese, or a cheese-based red sauce, studded with shrimps.

**2 Marides**
Tiny picarel are coated in flour, flash-fried and served with a slice of lemon and a dash of salt.

**3 Loukanika**
These smoked and spiced pork sausages are a typically Cretan snack, served more often in winter.

**4 Baked Potatoes**
Another typical winter snack served in mountain village *kafeneia*, often cooked in a wood-burning stove.

**5 Octopus (Ochtapodi)**
A favourite accompaniment to a glass of *ouzo* or *tsikoudia* is a dish of octopus chunks cooked in oil, herbs and vinegar. Alternatively, try a grilled tentacle.

**6 Kalitsounia**
Small baked turnovers stuffed with crumbly soft cheese and herbs, sometimes drizzled with honey.

**7 Askolymbroi**
Boiled baby golden thistle – served root and sprout – has a brief fresh season; later in the year it's only available pickled.

**8 Apaki**
Smoked lean pork tenderloin, best made from young suckling pigs. Easy to make, thus becoming more popular.

**9 Omathies**
A tasty rice and offal sausage, a local dish of eastern Crete.

**10 Melitzanosalata**
A savoury dip made by mashing grilled aubergines with garlic and chopped red pepper.

# 🔟 Markets and Shopping Streets

**Shop in an archaeological museum**

### 1 Museum Shops
MAP Q1

For quality replicas of finds from the archaeological sites of Crete, visit the Museum Shops in the former Venetian Loggia on Odos Paleologou in Rethymno, and in the Byzantine Museum in Chania.

### 2 Boutari Winery, Archanes
MAP K4 ▪ 70100 Archanes ▪ 28107 31617

The best wines from Crete (as well as from other parts of Greece) can be tasted and bought in this visitor centre at Crete's largest winery, built on the Fantaxometocho Estate (see p91) outside Skalani village.

### 3 Odos Skridlof, Chania
MAP B6

Running through the centre of the old quarter, this has been a street of saddlemakers and cobblers for centuries. These days, satchels, sandals and handbags abound.

### 4 Odos Daedalou, Heraklion
MAP T2

This pedestrianized lane is lined with fashion outlets and some major chains selling jewellery, and linen and cotton clothes to summer visitors.

### 5 Local Products Exhibition, Agricultural Co-operative Union of Sitia
MAP Q4 ▪ Myssonos 74 ▪ Open by appt: call 28430 29991

Promoting the produce of local farmers, this co-operative venture is worth visiting to see how the vines and olives of Crete are grown. It is also a good place for quality olive oil, wine and *raki* – Crete's favourite spirit.

### 6 Chania Market, Sofoklis Venizelos Square, Chania
MAP B6 ▪ Closed for renovation

The market building is a Chania landmark and bustles with vendors and shoppers. A visual feast and also the place to buy herbs, olive oil, dried fruit, honey and typical Cretan souvenirs, such as *brikia*, the tiny metal pots used to brew Greek coffee.

**Crowds browsing the stalls at the covered Chania Market**

### 7 Market next to Municipal Gardens, Rethymno
**MAP F3**

An open-air market takes place in a car park here every Thursday from 7am until 1pm. Stalls sell local produce, fruit and vegetables, cheese, honey, flowers and clothing. The same market is held on Saturday mornings in the square next to the bus station.

### 8 Odos 1866, Heraklion
**MAP T2–3**

This is Heraklion's main market street and a great place to shop for Cretan herbs and herbal teas. It also offers an insight into the Cretan diet – along with the olives, you will see buckets of live snails for sale.

**Coffee roasters in Odos 1866 street**

### 9 Odos Souliou, Rethymno
**MAP Q1–2**

Rethymno's upmarket shopping street is lined with stores selling copies of Minoan pottery, traditional Cretan pottery and modern ceramics, as well as colourful cotton and linen, lace and embroidery.

### 10 Odos Ethnikis Andistasis, Rethymno
**MAP Q2**

The most photogenic market in Crete spills out – as it has for centuries – from open-fronted shops and stalls along Odos Ethnikis Andistasis and around the Venetian Porta Guora. Go early in the morning, when it is in full cry with waiters bustling from stall to stall with coffee.

---

## TOP 10 TRADITIONAL SHOPS

**1 Kahraman, Chania**
**Kondilaki St, Old Town**
A traditional artisan shop selling different kinds of "worry beads".

**2 Domaine Economou, Sitia**
Red wine *(see p117)* that is made from unique Liatiko grapes of the region.

**3 O Armenis, Chania**
**Sifaka 14**
The best knife-dealer, fitting blades to personalized wood or horn handles.

**4 Ioannis Petrakis Icons Art Studio, Elounda**
Marvellous icons *(see p117)* in the style of the famed Cretan School.

**5 Union of Sitia Winery, Sitia**
**Km 1, Sitia–Agios Nikolaos Highway (E75)**
Wine and olive oil made from produce sourced from farmers and winemakers.

**6 Vardaxis, Rethymno**
**Panou Koronaiou 31, Old Town**
Superior ceramics, including plates, bowls, objets d'art and tiles of all sizes.

**7 Archaeological Museum of Chania Shop, Chania**
**Skra 15, Chalepa**
Replicas of Minoan and Hellenistic jewellery, statuary and ceramics.

**8 Liranthos, Rethymno**
**Arkadi 66**
Traditional Cretan musical instruments.

**9 Cretan Village Shops, Arolithos**
**Servili Tilissou**
Textiles, embroidery and ceramics by local artisans.

**10 Nikos Siragas, Rethymno**
**Petalioti 2, Old Town**
Artistic wood-turner known for his range of beautiful handmade bowls, vases and works of art.

**Artifacts at Nikos Siragas**

# TOP10 Crete for Free

### 1 Kerasma
When you eat at a traditional Cretan taverna, you are often offered a *kerasma* (complimentary dessert) – generally *halva*, *kormos* (chocolate loaf), fresh fruit or yogurt with honey – as well as a glass of *raki* (a potent spirit) at the end of your meal. These are "on the house" – a symbol of Cretan hospitality. However, observance of this custom in upmarket or touristy tavernas is patchy.

### 2 Falasarna Beach Sunsets
Few experiences can beat watching the sun setting over the sea at the end of a hot summer day, either lying on the beach or sitting at a relaxed waterside café. As the afternoon heat subsides, the sky takes on orange, pink and purple hues. Pure romance.

### 3 Drinking Water
Tap water in Crete is good to drink – jugs of water are brought to tables, free of charge, at all bars, restaurants and cafés. On the Samaria hiking trail, there are abundant springs of fresh, clean mountain water, too.

### 4 Beaches
Beaches are free if you take your own towel and just lie on the sand – you pay only if you want to hire a sun bed and parasol. For pebble beaches, you might want to buy a roll-up reed beach mat to put under your towel.

**Turquoise waters at Elafonisi beach**

**Rethymno's Archaeological Museum**

### 5 Museums and Archaeological Sites
Most museums and archaeological sites offer free entry on 6 March (in memory of Melina Mercouri), 18 April (International Monuments Day), 18 May (International Museums Day), 28 October (Oxi Day) and on the first Sunday of each month (Nov–Mar).

### 6 Churches
Greek Orthodox churches have dark interiors, with candles and incense creating an eerily beautiful ambience. Look in during a service to hear the priest chanting religious texts. Both men and women should be dressed respectfully, with knees and shoulders covered.

### 7 August Full Moon
On the night of the August full moon, the Greek Ministry of Culture organizes free entry to all major archaeological sites, which stay open until midnight or 1am, and even stage performances in the grounds. On Crete, these sites include Phaistos, Gortys and Malia.

### 8 Hiking Trails
While many hiking trails in Crete charge a small fee, such as the Samaria Gorge (the fee goes towards upkeep), some, like the E4 trail, are free. On some routes, you'll find wooden tables and benches where you can picnic, but bring water and sandwiches.

**Hiking the Samaria Gorge in summer**

### 9 European Music Day
www.europeanmusicday.gr
From 21–22 June each year (the summer solstice and the longest day of the year), European Music Day sees some free open-air concerts in various cities in Greece, including Chania and Agios Nikolaos on Crete.

### 10 Open-air Markets
All the larger towns host a street market, or laïki agora, with stalls stacked with colourful local seasonal fruit and vegetables, and cheap household goods. Crete supplies much of Greece with fresh produce.

---

**TOP 10 BUDGET TIPS**

**1** Avoid peak season, which extends from early July to early September, when prices tend to rocket.

**2** Look for cheap flights in May to June and September to October, when budget airlines are operating, but the island is wonderfully quiet.

**3** Most museums and archaeological sites across the island offer cheap admission to children, students with ID and pensioners.

**4** Some B&Bs and hotels offer decent discounts when you book a stay of a week or longer.

**5** Camping is an affordable alternative, with several camping sites on the island. Free camping is illegal, and fines are high.

**6** To best explore by car, rent a vehicle at one point and return at another; many companies no longer charge for one way hire.

**7** Eating out, you can make a meal of mezedes (starter platters), which are much cheaper and often more interesting than main courses.

**8** Breakfast on bougatsa, a savoury-cheese or sweet-cream pie. Locals recommend Kirkor's (see pp76–7).

**9** Omnipresent souvlaki and gyros make a tasty and nutritious takeaway meal in larger towns or resorts, and are cheaper than a sit-down dinner.

**10** In tavernas, drink barrel wine served by the carafe, rather than expensive bottled wine.

**Affordable dining at a taverna**

# 🔟 Festivals and Events

**Greek Orthodox priests praying at an open-air Easter Mass**

### ① Epiphany
**Islandwide ▪ 6 Jan**

In the Greek calendar, Epiphany ends the 12-day reign of mischievous spirits who run loose during Christmas. Ceremonial rites banish the spirits until the next year, and baptismal fonts, springs and wells are blessed by priests. In all seaside locales, young men dive for the honour of recovering a crucifix tossed into the harbour.

**Diving for the crucifix at Epiphany**

### ② Independence Day/Feast of the Annunciation
**Islandwide ▪ 25 Mar**

This national day commemorating the beginning of Greece's struggle for independence in 1821 is combined with the Feast of the Annunciation. There are religious processions and military parades, music and dancing.

### ③ Easter
**Islandwide ▪ Mar–Apr**

This is the Greek calendar's most important celebration. It is predominantly a family affair, focusing on the home, where spit-roasted goat or lamb is the highlight of a day of eating and drinking. Formal religious processions are led by elaborately-attired priests and are often followed by fireworks. In many towns and villages, Saturday night sees the shooting and burning of an effigy of Judas Iscariot.

### ④ St George's Day
**MAP F3 ▪ Asi Gonia ▪ 23 Apr**

Hundreds of shepherds bring their sheep anually to the church of St George in Asi Gonia village, near Rethymno. They seek their patron saint's blessings for a healthy flock and a prosperous season. In return the shepherds distribute free sheep's milk.

### ⑤ Mediterranean Festival
**MAP Q4 ▪ Sitia ▪ End Jun/early Jul**

Established in 2013, this is a big local world-music and jazz bash with three days and nights of free concerts and stalls selling handicrafts and local food. The venue is the Papies pedestrian zone on the waterfront.

### 6 Heraklion Summer Festival

**MAP K3 ■ Heraklion ■ Early Jul–early Sep**

Assorted concerts, plays and dance performances in various city venues, including old-town plazas and buildings.

### 7 Dormition of the Virgin Mary

**Islandwide ■ 14 & 15 Aug**

The Dormition of the Virgin Mary *(Kimisi tis Panayias)* is second only to Easter in importance, but it tends to be a much more public celebration. Church processions are followed by open-air eating and drinking in the churchyard or village square, which are followed by music and dancing.

### 8 Festival of Agios Titos

**MAP K3 ■ Heraklion ■ 25 Aug**

The biggest celebration to mark the day of Crete's patron saint takes place at Heraklion, where icons and relics are carried through the streets of the city with great pomp. The saint's day is also celebrated with masses and other religious events at churches across the island.

### 9 Chestnut Festival

**MAP B3 ■ Elos ■ Late Oct/ early Nov**

This festival marking the chestnut harvest is celebrated in the village of Elos in southwest Crete. Music, dancing, drinking and eating chestnut-based dishes all play a part.

### 10 Arkadi

**MAP G4 ■ Moni Arkadi ■ 7–9 Nov**

This patriotic gathering commemorates the freedom fighters of the 1866 uprising and the defenders of Moni Arkadi, who preferred to blow themselves up rather than surrender to the Ottoman forces *(see pp36–7)*.

**Bust of Moni Arkadi Abbot Gabriel**

**TOP 10 SAINTS**

**Modern mosaic portraying St Paul**

**1 Agios Pavlos (St Paul)**
The chapel of Agios Pavlos stands between Agia Roumeli and Loutro; his biblical landfall was on the South Coast, at Kali Limenes.

**2 Agios Nikolaos (St Nicholas)**
The patron saint of seafarers and fishers is honoured all around the coast of Crete.

**3 Agios Titos (St Titus)**
This follower of St Paul was ordained the first bishop of Crete.

**4 O Taxiarchis Michael (St Michael)**
The commander *(taxiarchis)* of the heavenly host is especially revered by combative Cretans.

**5 Agios Georgios (St George)**
St George is doubly popular as the patron of shepherds and a warrior saint.

**6 Agios Efstathios**
Efstathios (Stathis for short) is especially popular in southwest Crete, where many chapels and children bear his name.

**7 Agios Ioannis Theologos (St John the Divine)**
St John wrote the *Book of Revelations* on Patmos, but he is also venerated on Crete.

**8 Profitis Ilias (Prophet Elijah)**
Many mountain-top chapels for this prophet may originally have been dedicated to the sun-god Helios.

**9 Agioi Deka (Ten Saints)**
Ten Cretan martyrs killed for their faith by the Romans have had a church near Gortys named after them.

**10 Agios Ioannis Prodromos (St John the Baptist)**
St John is often shown in Orthodox art wearing a sheep-skin and having unruly hair, symbolizing his dwelling in the wilderness by the Jordan river.

# 🔟 Islands and Boat Trips

**Hiking on Imeri Gramvousa island**

### 1 Imeri Gramvousa
**MAP B1**

This pretty island crag just off the Gramvousa peninsula is crowned by a dramatic, crumbling castle. There are daily boat trips in season from Kissamos, and excursions through tour agencies in Chania.

### 2 Elafonisi
**MAP A4**

With its sandy beach and tropical blue lagoon, the tiny, low-lying island of Elafonisi *(see p63)* is barely separated from the Crete shoreline. Daily boat trips from Paleochora (May–Sep) take an hour each way.

**Elafonisi beach with its striking pink sand**

### 3 Gavdos
**MAP D6**

Europe's southernmost point, where a few simple guesthouses, tavernas and beaches welcome visitors. Boats sail in summer from Agia Roumeli, Paleochora, Sougia and Chora Sfakion; the journey time is 3 to 4 hours. Check the timetable at www.anendyk.gr.

### 4 Paleochora–Agia Roumeli
**MAP B4–C4**

The boat from Paleochora hugs the rugged south coast, calling in at the lazy resort of Sougia, before chugging along to Agia Roumeli, a cheerfully ramshackle village at the foot of the Samaria Gorge.

### 5 Agia Roumeli–Chora Sfakion
**MAP C4–D4**

After marching up and down the Samaria Gorge, your journey can be extended along the coast by hopping on one of several daily boats that potter eastwards. All end up at the small port of Chora Sfakion.

### 6 Chrysi

The island of Chrysi ("Golden"), named for its sandy beaches, is known locally as Gaidouronisi ("Donkey Island") because of the Cretan habit of retiring elderly donkeys to uninhabited islands. Daily boat trips from Ierapetra *(see p116)* take 45 minutes each way.

### 7 Dia
**MAP L3**

Uninhabited Dia is home to pristine waters, perfect for sailing, swimming and fishing. The island can be visited on a day trip from Heraklion or Hersonissos.

### 8 Koufonisi
**MAP Q6**

Walking paths and beaches attract boats from Makrygialos, and a ruined Roman amphitheatre attests to a time when the island grew rich from the trade in murex, a sea mollusc from which imperial purple dye was made.

**Sailing yachts anchored in Koufonisi**

### 9 Spinalonga

The island of Spinalonga *(see pp34–5)* is surrounded by a fortress. Daily boat trips venture here in summer from Plaka, Elounda and Agios Nikolaos – a trip of five, 20 and 35 minutes respectively.

### 10 Andikythira

This makes an offbeat stop-off between Crete and mainland Greece to the northwest. From July to September, two weekly ferries sail from Kissamos to Andikythira, its larger neighbour Kythira and Gythio on the mainland.

---

## TOP 10 WATERSPORTS

**Windsurfing, a popular sport**

**1 Windsurfing**
Boards are readily available for hire, and the best beaches are Falasarna, Chersonissos, Malia and Sitia.

**2 Snorkelling**
Crete's crystal waters, teeming with colourful fish, are ideal for snorkelling.

**3 Banana Rides**
Inflatable bananas, towed at high speed and carrying up to half a dozen riders, are popular in Malia and Hersonissos.

**4 Sea Biscuit Rides**
Similarly popular is the "sea biscuit", a tough inflatable ring for a single rider.

**5 Catamaran Sailing**
Catamarans can be hired by the hour or day at most resorts, with instruction available for novice sailors.

**6 Yacht Sailing**
Yachts can be chartered "bareboat" (without skipper or crew), fully crewed or with a skipper only.

**7 Scuba Diving**
Although archaeological sites and ancient shipwrecks are off-limits, there are good dives to several wrecks from World War II.

**8 Waterskiing**
Waterskiing, though expensive, is available at most of the bigger resorts.

**9 Waterparks**
Near Hersonissos, Acqua Plus is a playground of waterslides, waves and waterfalls. There are smaller water-parks near Heraklion (Watercity) and Chania (Limnoupolis).

**10 Canyoning**
Kourtaliotiko in Rethymno is a popular spot for canyoning. Crete has unique vertical canyons in different gorges.

# Crete Area by Area

**Whitewashed houses lining the sheltered harbour at Loutro**

# TOP 10 Central Crete

The landscapes of central Crete include beaches, rolling farmland and rugged mountains – among them, Crete's highest summit, Mount Ida, or Psiloritis. This was the heartland of Minoan civilization, and the most important Minoan ruins lie just south of the island's modern capital, Heraklion. Along the north coast are some busy resorts, while on the south coast, there are quieter places to enjoy a beach holiday.

**Boats at the harbour of Heraklion**

**CENTRAL CRETE**

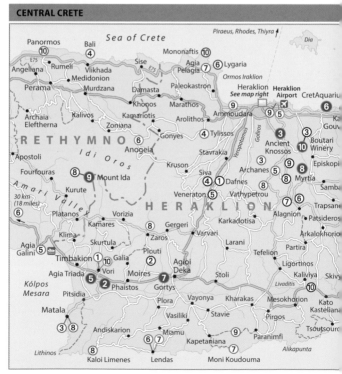

## 1 Heraklion

The modern capital of Crete was badly damaged during World War II, and only a few of its old Venetian buildings survived the reconstruction of the city. However, its Venetian fortress, harbour, arsenal and city walls are still impressive sights. The city's main and most popular attraction is the fascinating Archaeological Museum of Heraklion (see pp18–19).

## 2 Phaistos

This labyrinth of ruins dating from around 1600 BCE includes a Minoan courtyard and theatre with tiers of stone seats, a monumental stairway, peristyle hall and a vast central courtyard. The still undeciphered Phaistos Disc (see p19), which was discovered here, is on display in the Archaeological Museum of

**Ruins at the ancient site of Phaistos**

Heraklion. Phaistos was destroyed around 1450 BCE by the cataclysms that also laid low Crete's other Minoan palaces. Not usually as crowded as the more famous Knossos, the site at Phaistos (see pp24–5) has an impressive location on a hillside above fertile farmland.

| | |
|---|---|
| **1** | **Top 10 Sights** see pp89–91 |
| **1** | **Restaurants** see p97 |
| **1** | **Bars and Cafés** see p96 |
| **1** | **The Best of the Rest** see p92 |
| **1** | **Beaches** see p93 |
| **1** | **Outdoor Activities** see p94 |
| **1** | **Wineries** see p95 |

**Vivid fresco in the palace of Knossos**

### ⑤ Agia Triada

MAP H5 ■ 3 km (2 miles)
W of Phaistos ■ 28920 91564
■ Open 8:30am–3:30pm daily ■ Adm

Excavated in the early 1900s, Agia Triada is smaller than other Minoan sites such as Knossos and Phaistos, and was probably an aristocratic villa or a royal summer palace. Fine Minoan pottery discovered here, including three carved stone vases, is displayed in the Archaeological Museum of Heraklion. Agia Triada draws fewer visitors than the larger sites, so you can explore its honeycomb of stone corridors, stairs and courtyards at your own pace.

### ③ Ancient Knossos

Knossos was pinpointed as an important archaeological site by the great Heinrich Schliemann, and unearthed by British archaeologist Sir Arthur Evans, starting in 1900. The columns, courtyards and coloured frescoes of this ancient Minoan palace still have the power to amaze. Knossos (see pp12–15) was lost to history after the cataclysmic volcanic eruption that hastened the decline of Minoan civilization, but the site is now one of the island's most impressive relics of the vanished world of the Minoans.

### ④ Historical Museum of Crete

MAP S1 ■ Sofokli Venizelou 27, Heraklion ■ Open 9am–5pm Mon–Sat ■ Adm ■ www.historical-museum.gr

Spanning the centuries from the Byzantine period right up to World War II, exhibits at this fascinating museum in Heraklion include Venetian monuments, Orthodox church frescoes, traditional folk costumes and two paintings by El Greco.

### ⑥ CretAquarium

MAP K3 ■ Heraklion ■ Open 9:30am–7pm daily (Nov–Mar: to 4pm) ■ Adm ■ www.cretaquarium.gr

Situated just a 10-minute drive from Heraklion airport, this modern aquarium is home to around 2,500 sea creatures representing 200 Mediterranean species.

**Basilica of St Titus, Gortyna**

### ⑦ Gortys

Roman columns, a ruined Byzantine basilica, fortifications and remains of temples all hint at the past glories of this little-visited site. First settled in Minoan times, Gortys (see pp28–9) became one of the main cities of Doric Crete. Later a Roman provincial capital, it was one of Crete's most prosperous cities until it was sacked by Arab invaders in the 8th century CE.

---

#### THE KNOSSOS ENIGMA

Most archaeologists believe that the maze of ruins at Knossos was a royal palace, the bustling hub of the greatest empire that the islands of the Aegean had ever seen. But a few "heretical" archaeologists claim that Knossos may actually have been a giant necropolis where kings and nobles were interred, as in the tombs of ancient Egypt.

### 8 Kazantzakis Museum

MAP L4 ■ Myrtia village
square 9 ■ Open Apr–Oct: 9am–5pm
daily; Nov–Mar: 10am–3pm Mon–Fri &
Sun ■ Adm ■ www.kazantzaki.gr

Cretan author Nikos Kazantzakis
(1883–1957) is best-known for his
novel *Alexis Zorbas*, which was filmed
in 1964 as *Zorba the Greek*, starring
Anthony Quinn in the title role. The
author was born in Myrtia, and a
small museum in the Kazantzakis
family home is crammed with his
manuscripts and diaries, photos
and other memorabilia.

**Display at the Kazantzakis Museum**

### 9 Mount Ida

MAP H4

At 2,456 m (8,060 ft), Mount Ida
*(see p33)*, which is also known as
Mount Psiloritis, is Crete's highest
mountain. From the car-accessible
Nida Plateau, any fit and properly
shod mountain walker can undertake
the path climb up (allow 7–8 hours
including the return trip).

### 10 Boutari Winery and Audio-Visual Show

MAP K4 ■ Open 9am–5pm Mon–Fri, by
appt on weekends (Nov–Mar: 8:30am–
4:30pm) ■ Adm ■ www.boutari.gr

At the Fantaxometocho Estate, near
Archanes village, one of Greece's
leading winemakers has opened a
state-of-the-art audiovisual show
celebrating the island's landscapes,
history and way of life. The show also
highlights the vineyards and grape
varieties that produce some of the
Boutari family's award-winning wines.
You can sample and buy Boutari red
and white wines at the winery shop.

## A MORNING IN HERAKLION

▶ Start at the ornate Porta
Kenouria archway, once the
main entrance into the walled
city – Heraklion was fortified by
the Venetians to defend it against
the Ottoman Turks. Walk through
the gate and down Evans Street
to arrive on Platia Kornarou,
with its central six-sided stone
building, originally a pumphouse,
now a café. Next to it, the
Venetian Bembo Fountain
incorporates a headless marble
torso from a Roman statue.

Proceed north of the fountain,
along **Odos 1866** *(see p79)*, which
hosts Heraklion's daily market,
with stalls selling fresh fruit,
olives and nuts. Cross over
Plateia Nikiforou Foka to Plateia
Veniz-elou, lined with cafés and
centred on the 17th-century
**Morosini Fountain** *(see p16)*, with
four lions holding up the main
basin. Leave the square by 25
Augoustou Street, pass the
imposing Loggia (Venetian Town
Hall), then turn immediately right to
find **Agios Titos** *(see p17)*. Originally
Byzantine, this church was rebuilt
by the Venetians, turned into a
mosque by the Ottomans and later
reclaimed by the Orthodox Church
in 1925. A reliquary contains the
skull of St Titus.

Continue down 25 Augoustou to
the seafront, then walk along
the causeway to the **Venetian
Fortress** *(see p16)*. Having
explored the old town, either
follow the seafront promenade
west to the **Historical Museum** or
visit the **Archaeological Museum
of Heraklion** *(see pp18–19)* on the
east side of town.

*See map on pp88–9*

# The Best of the Rest

### 1 Museum of Cretan Ethnology, Vori
MAP H5

One of the first museums (see p51) to celebrate the lives of ordinary Cretans.

### 2 Palace of Malia
MAP M4

Only 3 km (2 miles) east of the bustling resort of modern Malia (see p42), this ruined Minoan palace once yielded fantastic treasures.

**Remains of the Palace of Malia**

### 3 Mount Giouchtas
MAP K4

To the south of Archanes, Mount Giouchtas is the mythical burial place of the god Zeus. The remains of a Minoan sanctuary are below the summit. Inhabited by eagles, vultures and other raptors, this has been declared a conservation area.

### 4 Minoan Villa Site, Tylissos
MAP J4 ■ 28108 31372 ■ Open 8am–3pm Tue–Sun ■ Adm

Tylissos was inhabited more than 4,000 years ago, but the most interesting discoveries are the remains of three large Minoan villas.

### 5 Archaeological Collection of Archanes
MAP K4 ■ 28107 52712 ■ Open 8:30am–3:30pm Wed–Mon ■ Adm

The small farming town of Archanes has a surprisingly good museum with finds from nearby sites, which include clay Minoan coffins, fragments of pottery, and a ceremonial dagger that may have been used in human sacrifice.

### 6 Church of Archangelos Michail, Asomatos
MAP K4

The Archangel Michael, leader of the heavenly host, is known in Greek as "O Taxiarchis" (the Brigadier) and is depicted in armour, sword in hand, along with other saints in the frescoes within this pretty 14th-century church at Asomatos.

### 7 Koudouma Monastery
MAP K6 ■ Open dawn to dusk daily ■ Donations welcome

The monks of Koudouma live in enviable isolation in a small monastery on a pebble beach, a long dirt-track drive down from Sternes village.

### 8 Vathypetro Minoan Villa
MAP K4 ■ 28102 26470 ■ Open Apr–Oct: 8am–3pm Tue–Sun; Nov–Mar: visit by appt

Vathypetro was presumably the home of a Minoan landowner, and ancient wine-making equipment found on the site indicates that the surrounding vineyards are thousands of years old.

### 9 Mount Kofinas
MAP K6

A mere hillock (see p65) by Cretan standards, but still a satisfying climb (starting from Kapetaniana village) with great views of Mount Ida and the south coast.

### 10 Venetian Fortress (Koules), Heraklion
MAP U1 ■ Old Harbour ■ Open 8:30am–7pm daily (Nov–Mar: to 3pm) ■ Adm

Known to the locals as the Koules, this sturdy 16th-century fortress (see p16) was built by the Venetians to protect Heraklion's harbour. It reopened in 2016 following restoration.

See map on pp88–9

# Beaches

**1 Malia**
MAP M4

A long strip of bars, clubs, shops, hotels and apartments lines the main coast highway at Malia. The splendid sandy beach is crowded with sun loungers and umbrellas from early summer until September.

**2 Hersonissos**
MAP M3

A big, brash resort that may soon grow to merge with neighbouring Stalida and Malia. The east beach is unarguably superb, and it has an excellent array of multinational bars and restaurants.

**3 Matala**
MAP G6

An open bay with coarse sand and pebbles, Matala first attracted sun-seeking hippy travellers in the 1960s, including Joni Mitchell who wrote the song *Carey* here. It soon graduated to become a small holiday resort in the 1980s.

**4 Bali**
MAP H3

A small, purpose-built resort set around three coves sheltered by cliffs.

**5 Agia Galini**
MAP G5

This former fishing village, now a seaside resort, is set by a crescent bay where a reed-lined river meets the sea. A day-trip will be needed to reach the beach.

**6 Dytikos (Lendas)**
MAP J6

One of the longest beaches on the south central coast, Dytikos is popular with naturists.

**7 Kato Gouves**
MAP L3

With its long stretch of sand and shingle and growing number of package holiday hotels, this is one of the better beaches close to Heraklion.

**8 Kaloi Limenes**
MAP H6

A relatively remote and peaceful series of small beaches and coves among dramatic cliffs. However, the offshore oil tanker terminal rather mars the view.

**9 Heraklion**
MAP K3

If you have time to kill while in the capital, head for the municipal beach at Amnissos, which is open from 9am to 7pm for a small fee.

**10 Panormos**
MAP G3

One of the less developed beaches on Crete's central north coast, Panormos has a small stretch of sandy beach beside a miniature fishing harbour and a handful of places to eat and drink.

**Swimmers in the turquoise waters near Agia Galini**

# Outdoor Activities

**Visitors inside the Dikteon Cave**

### 1 Hiking Crete
MAP M4 ▪ Malia
▪ www.hiking-crete.com

These half-day hiking tours whisk you into Crete's remote interior to explore the Roza Gorge, the Katharo Plateau or the Minoan Path, which ends at the Dikteon Cave.

### 2 Cycling Creta
MAP M4 ▪ Analipsi, Hersonissos
▪ www.cyclingcreta.gr

This company offers informative guided mountain-bike tours at various levels of difficulty. They cater for small groups and also offer free pick-up and drop-off from Heraklion, Gouves, Stalida and Hersonissos.

### 3 Enjoy Crete
MAP K3 ▪ Heraklion
▪ www.enjoy-crete.com

Sea-kayaking day and multi-day trips are arranged in either single or double kayaks, with instruction. The company also offers hiking tours for all ability levels.

### 4 Scubakreta
MAP M3 ▪ Hersonissos
▪ www.scubakreta.com

This is a well-equipped scuba diving outfit offering courses (PADI) and organized boat and shore dives from its centre in Hersonissos.

### 5 Sailing Trips Crete
MAP T1 ▪ Venetian Harbour, Heraklion ▪ www.sailingtrips.gr

Take a half-day trip aboard a sleek sailing boat (maximum 8 persons). Tours depart twice daily from Heraklion to the islet of Dia (see p85), with time for snorkelling, fishing and lunch.

### 6 Eurodiving
MAP K3 ▪ Ligaria beach, Agia Pelagia ▪ www.eurodiving.net

Scuba diving courses (PADI) for all levels, diving excursions and equipment for hire are all available here. Some 25 nearby dive sites include underwater caves and reefs.

### 7 Heraklion Diving Centre
MAP K3/L3 ▪ Efodou 25, Heraklion/Hersonissos ▪ www. heraklion-diving.com

Passionate, well established (since 1977), and professional diving instructors offer lessons at all levels, plus guided scuba-diving trips. Main sites, including a crashed German plane and Amphora Reef, are near Hersonissos.

### 8 Green Tour
MAP H4 ▪ www.greentour.gr

A one-day guided hike up Mount Ida (see p91), called "Crete from Above", is one of two day-long itineraries offered by this Rethymno-based company. The trip includes lunch at a shepherd's hut.

### 9 The Hub MTB Adventures
MAP M4 ▪ Malia ▪ www.mtbhub.gr

Taking you away from the crowds, into rural Crete, these mountain-bike excursions cover nearly a dozen off-road itineraries of all difficulties, including single-track.

### 10 Stay Wet Diving
MAP K3 ▪ Mononaftis beach, Agia Pelagia ▪ www.staywet.gr

A major advantage of this PADI-affiliated operator, especially for those who hate long boat rides, is the ability to dive straight off the beach.

# Wineries

**1 Douloufakis**
MAP J4 ■ Dafnes, 18 km
(11 miles) S of Heraklion
■ www.cretanwines.gr

Set amid lush vineyards and olive groves, Douloufakis was founded in 1930. Welcoming and knowledge-able, it runs tours and tastings of its award-winning wines.

**2 Zacharioudakis**
MAP J5 ■ Plouti, 48 km
(30 miles) SW of Heraklion
■ www.zacharioudakis.com

Near Gortys and the south coast, this modern, purpose-built hillside winery produces organic wines and is open for tours and tastings.

The wine-tasting facilities at Boutari

**3 Boutari**
The tour at Boutari (see p91) takes you through its vineyards and visitors then watch a short film about winemaking, followed by a tasting.

**4 Daskalakis**
MAP J4 ■ Siva Palianis,
17 km (10 miles) S of Heraklion
■ www.silvawines.gr

Located near Dafnes, this family-run business dates from 1890. All its wines are certified organic, and its Sauvignon Blanc is outstanding. Open for tours and tastings.

**5 Idaia**
MAP J4 ■ Veneraton, 18 km (11 miles) S of Heraklion ■ www.idaiawine.gr

This winery focuses on quality rather than quantity. Sample Idaia's award-

winning velvety red Ocean, its extra-dry single varietal Vidiano white or its Grenache Rouge rosé.

**6 Lyrarakis**
MAP L4 ■ Alagni, 18 km
(11 miles) S of Heraklion ■ www.lyrarakis.com

Credited with reviving the two ancient local white varieties, Daphni and Plyto, this winery dates from 1966 and offers informative tours and tastings with savoury snacks.

**7 Paterianakis**
MAP L4 ■ Alagni, 18 km
(11 miles) S of Heraklion ■ www.paterianakis.gr

With a hilltop tasting room that affords spectacular views over the surrounding vineyards, this welcoming winery prides itself on an all-organic product line.

**8 Minos Miliarakis**
MAP L4 ■ Peza, 17 km
(10.5 miles) S of Heraklion
■ www.minoswines.gr

Trading in its present form since 1932, this high-capacity winery makes wine from a wide variety of indigenous and imported grapes. Visits take in a small museum as well as tasting facilities.

**9 Stilianou**
MAP L4 ■ Kounavi,
12 km (7 miles) S of Heraklion
■ www.stilianouwines.gr

The mountain vineyards of this boutique winery produce limited quantities of organic wines, sold in numbered bottles. Stilianou is open all year for tastings.

**10 Strataridakis**
MAP L5 ■ Arkalochori,
33 km (20 miles) SE of Heraklion
■ www.strataridakis.gr

Now run by two brothers, this winery dates from 1955. Just a limited number of wines (8 labels) are currently produced.

See map on pp88–9 ←

# Bars and Cafés

**Outdoor tables and a fountain outside Mare Heraklion Riviera**

### 1 Mare Heraklion Riviera, Heraklion
MAP S1 ▪ Sofokli Venizelou ▪ 28102 41946

Located on the waterfront, Mare serves coffee and light snacks by day and cocktails by night. Enjoy the sunset on the café's lovely terrace.

### 2 The Bitters Bar, Heraklion
MAP T2 ▪ Stoa Platia Liontarion 25

In a covered arcade close to the Morosini Fountain, this bar serves morning coffee, plus an extensive range of expertly shaken cocktails.

### 3 Kirkor, Heraklion
MAP T1 ▪ Liontara Square

Start the day with a Cretan-style breakfast of coffee and a cream-filled *bougasta (see p76–7)* while enjoying the view of the Lion Fountain.

### 4 Pagopoieion, Heraklion
MAP T2 ▪ Platia Agios Titos ▪ 28102 21294

This bistro bar, housed in an old ice factory, hosts live music performances.

### 5 New York Beach Club, Hersonissos
MAP M3 ▪ 28970 23415

Enjoy breakfast, snacks and cold drinks during the day at this beach bar *(see p77)* by the harbour entrance, and party to the lively music at night.

### 6 Xalavro Open Bar, Heraklion
MAP T2 ▪ Milatou 10 ▪ 69456 99292

This old-fashioned bar and restaurant serves creative cocktails and fresh local cuisine.

### 7 Almyra Seaside, Agia Pelagia
MAP K3 ▪ On the beach ▪ 28108 11388

With sun beds and parasols for hire, this slick beach bar and restaurant serves creative Mediterranean fare and cocktails.

### 8 Port Side Bistro, Matala
MAP G6 ▪ Above the beach ▪ 694 5983 886

A café-bar right above the beach, Port Side serves snacks and drinks (alcoholic and soft) and often has a DJ event on Friday evenings.

### 9 Dish Bar, Heraklion
MAP T2 ▪ Papagiamali 3 ▪ 28102 227118

In a Neo-Classical building by Agios Titos, this bar-restaurant offers food, drinks and music till the early hours.

### 10 Ouzeri tou Terzaki, Heraklion
MAP T1 ▪ Ioannou Marineli 17 ▪ 28102 21444

This friendly taverna *(see p76)* offers a range of dishes.

# Restaurants

**PRICE CATEGORIES**
For a three-course meal for one with half
a bottle of wine (or equivalent meal),
taxes and extra charges.
.........................................................

€ under €25    €€ €25–40    €€€ over €40

### 1 Ippokampos, Heraklion
MAP S1 ▪ Sofokli Venizelou 3 ▪ €

On a terrace overlooking Heraklion's seafront promenade, this informal spot serves simple seafood dishes. Order grilled sardines, fried squid, a salad and a carafe of white wine – all tasty and reasonably priced, hence the queues.

### 2 Erganos, Heraklion
Georgiadou 5 ▪ 28102 85629 ▪ €

Savour traditional Cretan cooking in an appropriately folksy environment. Signature dishes include snails, lamb's liver, or sweetbreads and grilled mushrooms.

### 3 Kyriakos, Heraklion
Leoforos Dimokratias 53 ▪ 28102 22464 ▪ €

In traditional taverna style, you will be beckoned into the kitchen at this old-fashioned restaurant with smoke-stained, wood-panelled walls. Choose your meal from bubbling pots or glass cases filled with fish, chops and vegetables.

### 4 Kouzineri, Heraklion
MAP K3 ▪ Agiou Titou ▪ 28103 46452 ▪ €€

This steakhouse, known for its high-quality meat, boneless BBQ ribs and Kouzineri burgers with cheddar mashed potatoes and artichoke pie.

### 5 7 Thalasses, Heraklion
MAP K3 ▪ Irakleitou & Irodotou 1, Nea Alikarnassos ▪ 28103 42945 ▪ €€

This welcoming restaurant specializes in local seafood. Dine here on fresh fish, salad and a bottle of white wine. It lies east of town, near the airport.

### 6 Arodamos, Anogeia
MAP H4 ▪ Milopotamou, Upper village ▪ 28340 31100 ▪ €

A contemporary village taverna, Arodamos known for its hospitality, serves grilled lamb, local specialities and a variety of goat milk cheeses.

### 7 El Greco, Lendas
MAP J6 ▪ Above the beach ▪ 28920 95322 ▪ €€

Overlooking the Libyan Sea, El Greco (see p74) offers traditional food made with local ingredients, plus an extensive wine list. Reservations required.

### 8 Elia, Zaros
MAP J5 ▪ 1.5 km (1 mile) outside Zaros village ▪ 28940 31238 ▪ €€

Elia is the restaurant of the Eleonas Country Inn. All the standard dishes are served inside or outside, in a rustic wood-and-stone environment.

Charming dining terrace at Elia

### 9 Mourelo Cretan Cuisine, Ammoudara
MAP K3 ▪ Ikaros Apartments, Dios ▪ 28108 24838 ▪ €

This modern restaurant (see p75) offers a menu of traditional Cretan and Mediterranean fusion dishes.

### 10 Alekos, Vori
MAP H5 ▪ By Agia Pelagia church ▪ 28920 91094

Lovely courtyard-house taverna with food to match. Chef-owner Alekos has spent time in Belgium, which is reflected in his style of cooking.

*See map on pp88–9* ←

# TOP10 Western Crete

Much of western Crete is dominated by the jagged peaks of the Lefka Ori (White Mountains), which are often snowcapped until June. Traversed by spectacular gorges, the mountains drop sharply to the Libyan Sea on Crete's south coast. These mountains were for centuries the heartland of islanders' resistance to foreign occupiers. Many of the remoter villages were accessible only on foot until the second half of the 20th century, and a traditional way of life lingered longer here than in other parts of the island. The west also has Crete's two most attractive towns, Chania and Rethymno, and some of the best beaches, ranging from pebbly coves to long swathes of golden sand.

**Rethymno's fortress**

## WESTERN CRETE

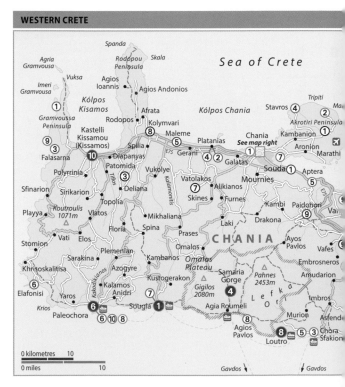

*Previous pages The Dikteon Cave, said to be the birthplace of Zeus*

**The rugged coastline around Sougia**

An hour's walk away, the ruins of the ancient city-state of Lissos can be found, including a temple to the healing god Asclepius. It has a mosaic floor which dates from the 3rd century BCE.

### ① Sougia
MAP C4

Sougia is perfect for anyone in search of peace, quiet and isolation. Tourism is very low-key, with just a scattering of small pensions and guesthouses, tavernas and cafés. The town's beach is long and pebbly, and the water is sparklingly clear.

### ② Rethymno

Rethymno is Crete's third-largest town (after Heraklion and Chania) and its most attractive, with an inner harbour overlooked by a huge, brooding Venetian fortress (the Fortezza), streets of old-fashioned Venetian mansions, and a palm-fringed esplanade along a sandy beach. Thanks to its nearby beaches, Rethymno *(see pp26–7)* has become a fully fledged resort town, with holiday hotels east of the city centre, and plenty of shops, restaurants, bars and cafés. It also has colourful early morning markets on Thursday and Saturday.

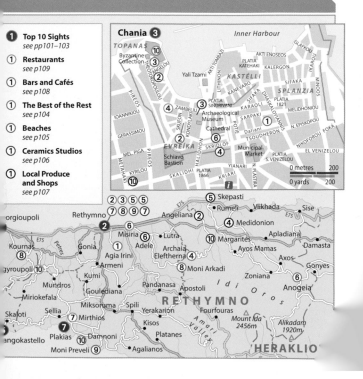

**Chania ③**

### 3 Chania

Chania, Crete's second-largest city, is built around a natural harbour that attracted many settlers over the millennia, from Minoans to Romans, Byzantines, Saracens, Venetians and Ottomans. The old town, a huddle of narrow streets, is well sown with bars, restaurants, shops and museums. Chania *(see pp20–21)* has some of Crete's most spectacular scenery as a backdrop, with the slopes of the Lefka Ori (White Mountains) rising steeply a short way inland and dominating the entire southern horizon.

**The mosque in the Old Port at Chania**

### 4 Samaria Gorge

Taking its name from the tiny Venetian-era church of Osia Maria, this is probably Crete's most dramatic stretch of scenery. The gorge *(see pp30–31)* cuts its way through the Lefka Ori from the Omalos Plateau to the Libyan Sea, and narrows to a width of only a few arm widths at its narrowest point. The gorge lies within the Samaria National Park, a refuge for many rare birds, plants and mammals.

### 5 Frangokastello

MAP E4

A small "Castle of the Franks", actually built by the Venetians to defend this stretch of the south coast against pirate attacks *(see p46)*, gives this small resort its name. Frangokastello has two separate sandy coves, and offers, by way of accommodation, small pensions and apartments. A handful of restaurants and cafés cater to visitors, and goat and lamb dishes regularly feature on the menus.

### 6 Paleochora

MAP B4

Paleochora stands on a peninsula between a long sandy bay to the northwest and an even longer, but pebblier beach to the southeast. Just beyond the village, on a cape, loom the ruined walls of Venetian fort Castel Selino, built to guard the harbour and coast but left to crumble after the Ottoman conquest. Paleochora is one of Crete's quieter resorts, with a low-key nightlife and a family atmosphere.

### 7 Plakias

MAP F4

Plakias's excellent beaches were overlooked by the holiday industry until the late 1980s, when the tiny fishing community became a strip of hotels, apartments, shops and restaurants. Plakias has plenty going for it, including attractive surrounding countryside, a long sweep of shingly sand, and other, even prettier beaches and palm-fringed coves within walking distance.

### 8 Loutro

MAP D4

Snugly hemmed in by cliffs rising steeply just inland, Loutro is one of the most charming spots on Crete. Dazzling white pensions and apartments sit above the tiny crescent-shaped beach. Accessible only on foot (by a precarious cliff path) or by boat from Chora Sfakion, Loutro is ideal for a relaxing holiday – without sandy beaches.

## INDOMITABLE COUNTRY

The Sfakia region lived by its own laws for generations, and vendettas between local families were not uncommon, even a couple of generations back. Prosperity and communications have tamed the region somewhat, but some Sfakiots still have an illicit firearm or two hidden away in the attic – and in the remoter parts, it seems that no road sign has escaped target practice.

## A MORNING IN RETHYMNO

Begin your day at Plateia Tessera Martyron, where **Porta Guora** (see p27) – the only intact remnant of the Venetian city walls – leads into the old town. Pass through the gate and walk north along Ethnikis Anistasis, where the market bustles with stalls, open-fronted shops and cafés. This is a great place to buy herbs, honey and olive oil. This street ends beside the **Nerantzes Mosque** (see p26), converted from a Venetian church, as can be seen from the ornate northern portal. Its slender minaret can be seen from some distance.

At Nerantzes, turn left onto Vernardou and midway along, on your left, step into the **Historical and Folk Art Museum** (see p50), displaying textiles and traditional costumes. Next, turn right on Epimenidou, then again right onto Arabatzoglou, which leads down to Petihaki, a small square where you'll find the **Rimondi Fountain** (see p27), built in 1627 to supply the town with drinking water. Nearby, the elegant 16th-century **Loggia** (see p27) is a poignant reminder of Venice's reign.

Continue along Mesolongiou, past the Catholic church of **St Anthony of Padua**, then onto Himaras to the **Rethymno Archaeological Museum** (see p49), which displays Neolithic, Minoan and Roman finds. Cross Katehaki to the **Fortezza** (see p26). This fortress was built by the Venetians in 1573 to protect against invasion, but in the end it proved no match for the Ottomans, who merely skirted it to take the city. End with a seafood lunch at one of the quayside tavernas at the Venetian Harbour.

## Georgioupoli
### MAP E3

Founded little over a century ago, this town was named in honour of Prince George, the then-governor of Crete. It is now a resort, with hotels stretching along the sandy beach. Georgioupoli attracts a less raucous clientele than resorts such as Malia and Hersonissos. At its heart is a town square, shaded by eucalyptus trees, while nearby a river meets the sea.

## Kissamos
### MAP B2

Formally known as Kastelli Kissamou, Crete's westernmost town is tucked away in a bay between the Rodopou and Gramvoussa peninsulas. There are several rarely visited ancient and medieval sites nearby, including Polyrrinia (see p47), plus an excellent archaeological museum (see p48). There are also pleasant (if unexceptional by Cretan standards) beaches on either side of town.

**Whitewashed houses in Loutro**

*See map on pp100–101* ←

# The Best of the Rest

### 1 Monastery of Agia Irini
MAP F3 ▪ 28310 27791
▪ Open 9am–8pm daily (Nov–Mar: to 6pm)

This 14th-century monastery is now a nunnery and also a centre for traditional weaving and needlework.

### 2 Akrotiri Peninsula
MAP D2

Monks have been drawn to Crete's peninsulas – Akrotiri's best monasteries are the abandoned Moni Katholiko and the Venetian Moni Agias Triadas Tzangarolon *(see p45)*.

### 3 Chora Sfakion
MAP D4

A major rendezvous point for excursion groups who arrive by boat having walked the Samaria Gorge. Once they return to their coaches, the town reverts to its pleasant slumber.

### 4 Ancient Eleftherna
MAP G3 ▪ Open 8:30am–7pm daily ▪ www.en.mae.com.gr

Founded in 700 BCE, ancient Eleftherna was a powerful Dorian city. Having vanished from history, it is now being rediscovered by Greek archaeologists.

### 5 Aptera
MAP D2 ▪ Open 8:30am–3pm Wed–Mon

In this Byzantine town built on the site of a Hellenistic city, there are remains of Roman cisterns, a Venetian monastery and an Ottoman fort.

### 6 Anogeia
MAP H4

Cafés and shops conceal Anogeia's embattled past, when it was a hotbed of resistance – first against the Ottomans, then the Germans.

### 7 Souda Bay War Cemetery
MAP D2

The burial place of more than 1,500 Commonwealth soldiers who died in the Battle of Crete in May 1941.

### 8 Moni Arkadi
MAP G4

This 16th-century monastery *(see pp36–7)* combines Cretan vernacular and Baroque architecture and includes an ornate Venetian church.

### 9 Ancient Falasarna
MAP A2 ▪ Falasarna
▪ Open 8:30am–3:30pm Wed–Mon

The ancient ruins of this former Dorian naval city estate are worth a visit. The closed Phoenician-style harbour is the most remarkable.

### 10 Maritime Museum of Crete
MAP A5 ▪ Akti Koundourioti, Chania
▪ Open 9am–5pm Mon–Sat, 10am–6pm Sun (Nov–Apr: 9am–3:30pm daily) ▪ Adm ▪ www.mar-mus-crete.gr

Navigational tools, model ships and naval equipment trace Crete's history in the sea in the Firkas fortress *(see p21)*.

**A Turkish fortress at ancient Aptera**

# Beaches

### 1 Balos
MAP B1

This pale-pink sand beach looks onto a shallow turquoise lagoon. Most visitors reach it by organized boat trips. Alternatively, drive along a pot-holed track from Kalyviani – a slow speed jeep is essential.

The beach and lagoon at Balos

### 2 Platanias
MAP C2

This is a good long beach within easy reach of Chania, offering plenty of places to eat and drink. Platanias is Chania's after-dark summer playground, packed with bars and clubs.

### 3 Falasarna
MAP A2

This long sweep of yellow sand is one of the finest on the west coast. The archaeological site at the north end helps control development, but there are plenty of tavernas and places to stay midway along the beach.

### 4 Stavros
MAP D2

Quieter than Platanias, making it an attractive alternative for those seeking a little tranquillity. This lagoon-like bay on Akrotiri Peninsula featured in the film *Zorba the Greek*.

### 5 Glyka Nera (Sweet-water Beach)
MAP D4

A tiny patch of pebble and sand, Glyka Nera takes its name from the fresh, potable water which wells up wherever you dig. It is reachable only by scrambling along a rough path (part of the E4), or by boat from Loutro or Chora Sfakion. Naturists favour this beach.

### 6 Elafonisi
MAP A4

The beach opposite the island of Elafonisi on the west coast is one of Crete's best, with a long crescent of white sand and shallow turquoise water that quickly warms in summer. It is very popular and is often busy.

### 7 Sougia
MAP C4

Shaded in places by a line of tamarisk trees, Sougia is one of the last alternative resorts in Crete, with free camping and nudism at the beach's east end, but enough space for all persuasions along its mile-plus length.

### 8 Agios Pavlos
MAP F5

A popular day-trip from Agia Galini, Agios Pavlos's main cove is not as impressive as the west beach, which is approached by descending Crete's largest sand dune.

### 9 Preveli Beach
MAP F5

The Kourtaliotis river meets the sea below Moni Preveli, where the green river, blue sea, Cretan palms and "Greek bamboo" (calamus reeds) create an oasis-like feel.

### 10 Damnoni
MAP F4

Damnoni's golden sands have been somewhat marred by insensitive hotel building. However, east of the main beach are two charming sandy coves, Ammoudaki and Mikro Ammoudaki, both popular with naturists.

*See map on pp100–101* ←

# Ceramics Studios

Ceramic items at Tetraktis Studio

## 1 Tetraktis Studio
MAP D2 ■ Verekynthos 6, Souda Chania ■ www.tetraktis-studio.gr

Yiannis Vlavogilakis makes board games from ceramics – draughts, dominoes and solitaire – as well as tiles and dozens of drums.

## 2 Ourios Ceramics
MAP C5
■ Theotokopoulou 4, Chania
■ www.ouriosceramics.gr

Babis Magdalinos creates ceramic ornaments with decorative details inspired by Greek folk art, and innovative glazes made from recycled glass bottles.

## 3 Flakatoras Ceramics
MAP B5 ■ Zampeliou 19, Chania
■ 6980 909010

This family-run studio and shop makes and sells hand-painted cups, plates and tiles, plus quirky colourful ornaments such as model fish, snails and penguins.

## 4 Michael Laventzakis
MAP B6 ■ Skrydlof 38, Chania
■ www.laventzakisceramics.gr

With designs inspired by Greek folk art, this family business produces functional and decorative teapots, cups, bowls and plates in 16 colours.

## 5 Apostolakis
MAP C2 ■ Maleme, 16 km (10 miles) W of Chania ■ 28210 62438

Costas Apostolakis creates ceramic cups, bowls, jugs, vases and candle-holders glazed in warm shades of orange, red, blue or green.

## 6 Melody Ceramics
MAP B6 ■ Mpetolo 27, Chania

Visit this studio and shop to purchase colourful handmade ceramics, including ornamental model boats, seagulls, flowers and pomegranates.

## 7 Vardaxis Ceramics
MAP P2 ■ Panou Koronaiou 31, Rethymno

George Vardaxis's plates, bowls, vases and tiles are hand-painted. His family have been making them for generations – his grandfather has works displayed in Athens Greek Folk Art Museum.

Figurine, Ourios Ceramics

## 8 Terra-Cotta
MAP E3 ■ Kournas
■ www.terra-cotta.gr

This family-run business makes beautiful oven-proof, dishwasher-safe kitchenware – plates, bowls, goblets and jugs – in 12 different glaze colours.

## 9 Manousos Chalkiadakis
MAP D3 ■ Paidochori
■ www.greekceramics.gr

In a renovated 18th-century house, Manousos's studio is open daily to visitors. You can buy his handmade ceramics here, and he also runs one-day ceramics courses.

## 10 ea Ceramics Studio
MAP G3 ■ Margarites, 27 km (17 miles) E of Rethymno ■ www.eaceramicstudio.com

Margarites is known for its centuries-old potteries. In their studio, Ema and Aris create funky modern handcrafted tableware – cups, jugs and bowls.

See map on pp100–101

# Local Produce and Shops

### 1 Moni Agia Triada
**MAP D2 ■ Akrotiri Peninsula**

Visit Moni Agia Triada's monastery (see p45), near Chania, then buy extra-virgin olive oil and organic wine made by chemists and winemakers.

### 2 Athos Workshop
**MAP G3 ■ Angeliana, 23 km (14 miles) E of Rethymno**
**■ www.athosworkshop.com**

This small company makes olive oil-based soaps – visit to see demonstrations and to buy soaps, herbal extracts and creams at its shop.

**Soap, Athos Workshop**

### 3 Astrikas Estate Biolea
**MAP C2 ■ Astrikas ■ www.biolea.gr**

In the hills behind Kolymvari, Biolea offers guided tours of the mill, an audio-visual presentation and olive-oil tastings. It also sells organic citrus-flavoured olive oil.

### 4 Paraschakis Olive Oil
**MAP G3 ■ Melidoni Geropotamou, 27 km (17 miles) E of Rethymno ■ www.paraschakis.gr**

This family-run farm offers an olive-oil tour including the history of olive-oil production, plus oil for sale.

### 5 Klados
**MAP G3 ■ Skepasti, 25 km (16 miles) E of Rethymno**
**■ www.kladoswinery.gr**

Tours here include a walk through the vineyard and a winemaking presentation, followed by wine-tasting (a handful of labels). There is also the chance to buy bottles.

### 6 Agreco Farm
**MAP F3 ■ Adele, 7 km (4 miles) E of Rethymno ■ www.agreco.gr**

Visit this welcoming farm shop to purchase beautifully packaged, locally-made Agreco olive oil, plus the farm's own Eau de Grece toiletries.

### 7 Manousakis
**MAP C2 ■ Vatolakos, 15 km (9 miles) SW of Chania**
**■ www.manousakiswinery.com**

This boutique winery offers tours and tastings, with an optional lunch, plus excellent organic wine and *tsikoudia* (a fragrant, clear grape spirit) to purchase.

### 8 Terra Creta
**MAP C2 ■ Kolymvari, main highway 24 km (15 miles) W of Chania ■ www.terracreta.gr**

This large-scale olive-oil producer runs tours of the mill followed by tastings and a chance to buy its award-winning extra-virgin olive oil and balsamic vinegar.

### 9 Dourakis
**MAP E3 ■ Alikampos**
**■ www.dourakiswinery.gr**

Open for informative tours and tastings, this award-winning winery lies in the fertile Apokoronas region, about halfway between Chania and Rethymno, and produces nearly a dozen reds, whites and rosés.

### 10 Abea Deli Shop
**MAP A6 ■ Skalidi 116, Chania**
**■ www.abea.gr/en/deli-shop**

Founded in 1889, Abea Deli stocks its own olive oil and natural olive oil-based soaps and cosmetics. Beautifully packaged, they make fine gifts.

**Items on display at Abea Deli Shop**

# Bars and Cafés

**Diners and musicians at a street lined with cafés, Paleochora**

### 1 Mylos, Platanias
MAP C2 ▪ Platanias Beach
▪ www.myloschania.com

A beachside club, Mylos is one of the prime summer-night destinations for local youth, with DJs and theme parties.

### 2 Sinagogi Bar, Chania
MAP A5 ▪ Alley off Kondylaki, Old Harbour

This popular bar is set in the large courtyard of a Venetian ruin. Corner sofas and quiet music provide a low-key vibe.

### 3 Fagotto Jazz Bar, Chania
MAP A6 ▪ Angelou 16

Chania's locals have been coming to Fagotto for a late-night drink, accompanied by occasional live jazz, since 1978. It is in Topanas district, and may open only after 10pm.

### 4 Kibar: To Monastiri Tou Karolou, Chania
MAP B6 ▪ Daliani 22

Kibar, in the courtyard of a former monastery, serves cocktails into the early hours. There are occasional DJ events, and even an art gallery.

### 5 Garden of Ali Vafi, Rethymno
MAP Q2 ▪ Tzane Bouniali 65

In a beautiful courtyard setting, this lantern-lit bar-restaurant offers drinks, snacks and hookah pipes, plus one weekly evening concert by established musicians.

### 6 Agios Bar, Paleochora
MAP B4 ▪ Eleftheriou Venizelou 1 ▪ www.agiosbar.gr

Housed in an imaginatively redesigned former industrial building, this hip café-bar serves its own coffee blends and cocktails with *raki* and *tsikoudia*.

### 7 To Halikouti, Rethymno
MAP Q2 ▪ Katehaki 3 and Melissou ▪ 28310 42632

Situated below Rethymno's historic fortress, this family-friendly café is a great place for coffee, a glass of wine, a light lunch or after-dinner drinks.

### 8 Meli, Rethymno
MAP Q2 ▪ Plateia Petihaki

The best natural goat's milk ice cream in Rethymno Old Town. Sit at a table by the adjacent Rimondi Fountain, or buy a cone if you are on the go.

### 9 Cul de Sac, Rethymno
MAP Q2 ▪ Plateia Petihaki
▪ 28310 26914

Close to the Rimondi Fountain, Cul de Sac is the perfect place for people-watching over a coffee or a cocktail.

### 10 Café Cosmogonia, Paleochora
MAP B4 ▪ Strovlon-Paleochoras 28
▪ 69867 70686

Just off Paleochora's central crossroads, Cosmogonia is the village's liveliest late-night joint. Great music, good vibes and friendly company guaranteed.

# Restaurants

**PRICE CATEGORIES**

For a three-course meal for one with half a bottle of wine (or equivalent meal), taxes and extra charges.

€ under €25 ■ €€ €25–40 ■ €€€ over €40

**1 The Five Restaurant, Chania**

MAP A6 ■ Akti Papanikoli 15, Neachora ■ 28210 86596 ■ €€

A local favourite in a seaside setting, The Five *(see p72)* is known for its creative Greek cuisine, with dishes such as Cretan carbonara and sardine bruschetta. Try the Pavlovaki dessert.

**2 Veneto, Rethymno**

MAP Q2 ■ Epimenidou 4 ■ 28310 56634 ■ €€

Amid 14th-century vaults beneath the Veneto Hotel, enjoy Cretan specials *(see p73)* such as fennelled snails and couscous, stamnagathi and artichoke fricasee, or *chtapodi krasato*.

**3 Avli, Rethymno**

MAP Q2 ■ Xanthoudidou 22 ■ 28310 26213 ■ €€€

Expect creative Cretan recipes *(see p72)* and simple cheese-based platters. Tables occupy a pretty garden setting.

**Picturesque courtyard setting at Avli**

**4 Tamam, Chania**

MAP B5 ■ Zambeliou 49 ■ 28210 96080 ■ €€

Try Tanam's Cretan and Levantine fusion dishes such as fennel fritters or rabbit in rosemary-wine sauce *(see p72)*.

**5 Prima Plora, Rethymno**

MAP Q2 ■ Akrotiriou 4 ■ 28310 56990 ■ €€€

This restaurant and wine bar *(see p72)* focuses on serving quality, organic food and local wine. Try the excellent sushi.

**6 Taverna tou Zisis, Rethymno**

MAP Q2 ■ Machis Kritis 63, Misiria ■ 28310 28814 ■ €

On the old Heraklion highway, 4 km (2 miles) east of Rethymno, Zisis' *(see p74)* charcoal-grilled lamb and chicken dishes are worth the trip from town.

**7 Plateia, Mirthios**

MAP F4 ■ Mirthios village ■ 28320 31560 ■ €

Traditional Cretan food, friendly staff and superb sea views *(see p74)* guarantee diners a good time.

**8 Methexis Paleochora**

MAP B4 ■ Paleochora ■ 28230 41431 ■ €€

Methexis *(see p72)* serves generous dishes such as lambs-liver roulade and *askolymbri* (golden thistle).

**9 Ta Douliana, Douliana**

MAP E3 ■ Centre of Douliana, on road between Kalyves and Vamos ■ 28250 23380 ■ Closed Mon ■ €€

Enjoy legendary Cretan cuisine, at this pretty taverna *(see p74)*, including dishes cooked in the traditional *xylofournos* wood oven.

**10 Taverna Arxaia Lappa, Argyroupoli**

MAP E4 ■ Argyroupoli ■ 28310 81004 ■ €€

Come for the traditional grilled meat dishes at this taverna *(see p74)*.

*See map on pp100–101* ←

# TOP 10 Eastern Crete

Crete's far east sees fewer holiday-makers, mainly due to its distance from the island's airports. The area's largest town Agios Nikolaos, however, is a thriving holiday resort, and Crete's most exclusive hotel and villa complexes can be found around Elounda. The east also has good beaches, notably the famous palm beach at Vaï, and Minoan ruins at Gournia, Mochlos and Zakros.

**Pristine waters around Elounda**

### 1 Elounda
MAP N4

Elounda is Crete's most expensive resort area, with many exclusive villa and hotel complexes, several of which have private beaches. The simple village has a cluster of shops and restaurants around a small fishing harbour. In summer, boats depart daily on trips to Spinalonga, the Venetian fortress-island.

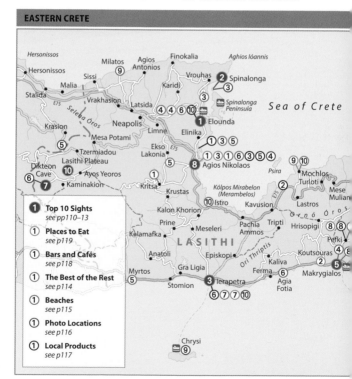

**EASTERN CRETE**

**Remains of Spinalonga's fortress**

### 2 Spinalonga
MAP N4

The fortification covering this small, rocky island *(see pp34–5)* at the entry to the Gulf of Mirabello was built by the Venetians in 1579 to control the approaches to this natural harbour. Venice managed to hang on to Spinalonga for half a century after the fall of the rest of Crete to the Ottomans, and it was surrendered only in 1715. It was used as a leper colony during the first half of the 20th century.

### 3 Ierapetra
MAP N6

Ierapetra is the largest town on the southeast coast. Aside from a tiny old quarter, it is rather dull, but has a good, long beach of grey sand and the distinction of receiving more hours of sunshine per year than anywhere else in Europe. Tomatoes and cucumbers are grown all year round in the surrounding farmlands. Ierapetra became an important Dorian Greek settlement in the 8th century BCE, and by the 2nd century BCE, it was the largest city-state on the island. Under the Romans, it was an important seaport; the Venetians built a fortress to defend the harbour. Today, the main sight is the archaeological museum.

### 4 Sitia
MAP Q4

Sitia looks surprisingly modern but was founded in the 4th century, when a thriving Byzantine city stood here. In the 14th century, it was damaged by earthquakes and sacked by pirates, and its fortunes waned. It was not until the late 1800s that Sitia became an important commercial centre. Its picturesque harbour is overlooked by a Venetian fortress and an Archaeological Museum *(see p49)*. Sitia is an important centre for the production of quality Cretan wines.

**Palm-lined promenade at Sitia**

**THE CAVES OF CRETE**

About 5,000 caverns and potholes riddle the island's mountain slopes. Grottoes have yielded fascinating relics of the ancient world, indicating that Crete was inhabited for thousands of years before the rise of the Minoan civilization. Only a handful have been fully charted, and thousands more remain to be fully explored and mapped.

### 5 Makrygialos
MAP Q5

Makrygialos is a popular holiday resort on Crete's south-eastern coast, with a long, straggling array of small pensions, hotels and tavernas stretching along a crescent of wind-swept, gently shelving sand and pebble beach, which is one of the best in this part of the island.

### 6 Zakros Gorge
MAP R5

The Zakros Gorge is known locally as the Valley of the Dead (see p65) because the caves in its limestone walls were used as tombs in Roman times. The gorge runs from the peaceful village of Ano ("upper") Zakros to Kato ("lower") Zakros on the sea, near an ancient Minoan palace site excavated in 1961. It is a beautiful hour-and-a-quarter hike uphill (allow an hour to walk back down).

### 7 Dikteon Cave
MAP M5

According to ancient Greek myths, this mossy cavern filled with strange limestone formations was the cradle of the greatest Olympian god, Zeus.

Rock formations in the Dikteon Cave

Rhea, Zeus's mother, supposedly hid the young godling from his father, Kronos, here. Bronze figurines and Minoan double axes found in the cave are on show in the Archaeological Museum of Herklion. The site is also often referred to as the Psychro Cave.

### 8 Agios Nikolaos
MAP N4

Set by the Gulf of Mirabello, Agios Nikolaos has the most attractive location of any town in eastern Crete. It is built around an inner lagoon, Voulismeni, surrounded by palm trees and pleasant cafés. Modern hotels and apartments now dwarf the surviving older buildings, but it is still a place of considerable charm. There are two small town beaches, and boats take holiday-makers to

larger beaches nearby. The town takes its name from the tiny 11th-century church of Agios Nikolaos (which now stands at the back of the Minos Palace Hotel).

###  Vaï
MAP R4

The beach at Vaï is famous for having the only wild palm grove in Europe. It is believed that Arab sailors planted the trees during historical times. However, both claims are spurious, as groves of this variety can be found around Crete, and elsewhere in the Aegean. The species, Phoenix Theoprasti, was first described by the 4th-century-BCE botanist, Theophrastos, in whose honour it was named. Today, the palm trees are fenced off and protected. The beach becomes overcrowded in high season, and it is better to visit outside the busiest summer months.

###  Lasithi Plateau
MAP M4

The so-called "Plain of Windmills" is a high plain of fertile farmland surrounded by bare limestone hills. Its nickname is misleading, though. Nowadays, rusting metal derricks outnumber the famed white-sailed windmills that once dotted the plateau in their hundreds. However, Lasithi is still well worth a visit for the spectacular drive through the mountains and the glimpses it offers of the traditional Cretan way of life.

**Panorama of Agios Nikolaos**

## A DRIVE IN EASTERN CRETE

This 200-km (125-mile) round trip from **Agios Nikolaos** can be made in one full day, or over two days, with an overnight stop at **Zakros**. From Agios Nikolaos, take the coastal highway east to **Gournia** *(see pp42)* to explore the Minoan archaeological site. Continue east to **Sitia** *(see p111)*, founded by the Byzantines, destroyed in the 14th century and rebuilt by a local *pasha* (Ottoman governor) in the 19th century. It has a picturesque harbour, where you might stop for coffee, and an **Archaeological Museum** *(see p49)* displaying Minoan treasures.

Proceed east to **Moni Toplou** *(see p45)*, a 14th-century fortified monastery. Visit the monastery church to see the icons, and to buy olive oil from the monks. Continue to **Vaï** beach, backed by its famous palm forest, now a conservation area, on Crete's east coast. Lined with parasols and sun beds, this sandy beach is one place you must have a swim. Once refreshed, head south to Ano Zakros, then turn left and drive down a narrow winding road to the seaside village of Kato Zakros, with its pebble-and-sand beachfront lined by informal tavernas. Stop for a late lunch, or even stay the night. After Zakros, head via the scenic Ziros plateau to Crete's south coast, through **Makrygialos**, another remote yet worthwhile beach resort, and west to seaside **Ierapetra** *(see p111)*. Unlike most Cretan coastal towns, this resort's economy is based on farming rather than on tourism. From here, it's a 32-km (20-mile) drive back to Agios Nikolaos.

*See map on pp110–11* ←

# The Best of the Rest

### 1 Kritsa
MAP N5

Overlooked by Mount Kastelleos, Kritsa stands at the edge of a wide, fertile plain and is regarded as one of Crete's most important craft centres.

### 2 Praisos
Based on clay statuettes and inscriptions found at this site (see p43), archaeologists believe it was a post-Minoan Eteocretan city.

### 3 Cretan Olive Oil Farm
MAP N4 ▪ Agios Nikolaos
▪ www.cretanoliveoilfarm.com

Visit here to learn about traditional olive-oil production, and sign up to open-air cookery and pottery lessons.

### 4 Lithines
MAP Q5

Named after its founders, the noble Byzantine Litinos clan, Lithines has two 15th-century churches, Agios Athanasios and Gennisi tis Panagias.

**Ancient ruins at Lato**

### 5 Lato
MAP N4

Lato was a Dorian Greek city that flourished between the 7th and 3rd centuries BCE. With massive stone walls, it offers fine views over the Gulf of Mirabello. Modern-day Agios Nikolaos was Lato's port.

**Toplou Monastery, a local landmark**

### 6 Moni Toplou
This fortified monastery (see p45) was founded in the 14th century. Its massive walls were built to protect it from pirates.

### 7 Roussa Ekklisia
MAP R5

This pretty village is worth visiting for its superb view of Sitia bay. Large plane trees shade the village square, nurtured by the spring which flows from under the medieval Agios Nikolaos church.

### 8 Moni Kapsa
MAP Q6 ▪ Open 8:30am–midday & 4–7pm

A monastery that seems to merge into the cliffs, with the mummified body of a monk in its chapel.

### 9 Pefki Gorge
MAP P5

An enjoyable 4-hour walk from Pefki to Makrygialos will take hikers along a dry river bed of white pebbles that runs through a pine-lined canyon with interesting rock formations.

### 10 Mochlos
MAP P4

East of Agios Nikolaos, Mochlos is a fishing hamlet. Just off shore, a tiny island (also called Mochlos) was home to an ancient Minoan settlement – excavations have uncovered superb gold jewellery and precious vases.

➤ *See map on pp110–11*

# Beaches

### 1 Sitia
MAP Q4

Unlike most larger Cretan coastal towns, Sitia has a good beach on its doorstep that is great for windsurfing.

### 2 Xerocampos
MAP R5

A tiny hamlet with a series of small, sandy east-facing coves. One of the few coastal areas not overrun by tourists, but offering facilities.

### 3 Kouremenos
MAP R4

The strong breezes at Kouremenos make it a popular windsurfing spot, with best conditions during summer, usually in the afternoons.

### 4 Makrygialos
MAP Q5

A good beach on the southeast coast. There's a long strip of sand interspersed with pebbles shelves guiding you gently into deeper water.

### 5 Myrtos
MAP N6

An amiably unpretentious farming and fishing village with a long, south-facing shingle beach, which is far less crowded than most in eastern Crete, even in high summer.

### 6 Agia Fotia
MAP R4

The best beach between Makrygialos and Ierapetra, this sheltered sandy cove, backed by pine-forested hills, makes a great swim-and-lunch stop.

### 7 Chiona
MAP R4

This beach has a European Blue Flag for clean sand and water, as well as ample choice in tavernas just inland.

### 8 Kato Zakros
MAP R5

At the foot of the Zakros Gorge, Kato Zakros has a crescent of sand and a pebble beach, with a small fishing harbour and a handful of pensions and tavernas.

**The waterfront at Kato Zakros**

### 9 Milatos
MAP N4

A pebbly beach which is surprisingly uncrowded compared with the teeming resorts only a few kilo-metres to the west.

### 10 Voulisma
MAP P5

This beautiful sandy cove, the best of several east of the resort of Istro, offers sunbeds and sometimes a light surf in which to play.

**The azure waters of Voulisma beach**

# Photo Locations

**1 Vaï Sand Beach**
MAP R4
The best spot for photographing this stunning beach, lined with straw umbrellas and sloping into shallow turquoise waters, is from the viewing platform on the hill at the south end.

**2 Vaï Palm Groves**
Making up Europe's largest palm grove, the centuries-old dated palms that back Vaï beach *(see p113)* give it a tropical atmosphere. Take photos of the palms overlooking the beach and the forest.

**3 Spinalonga**
This Venetian island fortress *(see pp34–5)* offers visitors many excellent viewpoints for taking photographs. It looks most impressive seen from aboard a boat as you approach the island's shore.

**4 Agios Nikolaos**
The centrepiece of this town is Voulismeni *(see pp112–13)*, a former fresh-water lake that is now joined to the sea by a narrow channel to form the inner harbour. The best viewpoint is from the road above the lake.

**5 Lasithi Windmills**
High up on the Lasithi Plateau, you'll find many windmills – some of stone, some whitewashed and several restored, with their white sails turning *(see p113)*.

**6 Dikteon Cave**
This cave complex *(see p112)* features an impressive lower chamber, which contains a small lake and is filled with beautifully lit stalactites and stalagmites.

**7 Zakros Gorge**
Follow the path through this imposing steep-sided rocky gorge *(see p112)* to descend at Kato Zakros, on the coast. On the way, look out for orchids, goats and buzzards.

**8 Pefki Gorge**
MAP Q5
Inland, north of Makrygialos, this gorge is known for its natural springs and streams, and for the fragrant pine trees that give it its name.

**9 Chrisi Island**
MAP N6
Accessed by daily summer excursion boats that sail from Ierapetra and Makrygialos, this uninhabited island is made up of sand dunes and characterful, centuries-old juniper trees, giving way to a turquoise blue sea.

**10 Ierapetra Harbour**
This little south-coast port *(see p111)* is filled with traditional wooden fishing boats, painted in white, blue and red, and equipped with buoys and nets. The castle serves as a backdrop.

**Windmills on the Lasithi Plateau**

# Local Products

**1** **Cretan Olive Oil Farm**
This farm has a shop (see p114) selling its own excellent extra-virgin olive oil, olives and olive paté, sun-dried tomatoes, fig jam and handmade soaps. Ideal for a picnic.

**2** **Votania Pure Herbs of Crete**
MAP P5 ■ Kavousi beach, 26 km (16 miles) E of Agios Nikolaos ■ www.votania.com
Votania grows organic sage, oregano, thyme, rosemary, lavender and mint, and then sells the dried herbs for cooking, teas and cosmetics.

**3** **Art on Olive Wood**
MAP N4 ■ Ikosiogdois Oktovriou 22, Agios Nikolaos ■ 28410 25168
Since 1985, this lovely workshop has been crafting beautiful objects, including ornate candle holders and elegant figurines of trees, boats and animals made from olive wood.

**4** **Ktima Toplou**
MAP R4 ■ Moni Toplou, Sitia ■ 28430 29637
The vineyard at the 14th-century Moni Toplou monastery (see p45) has unique varieties of vines used to produce excellent dessert, red and white Greek and Cretan wines such as Assyrtiko, Liatiko and Syrah, among others.

**5** **Melissa Traditional Products**
MAP N4 ■ Koundouros Roussos 18, Agios Nikolaos ■ 2841 024628
Visit this wonderful workshop (which was founded in 1973) and two shop-fronts for gorgeous handmade leather bags, sandals, belts and accessories, all made with classic Crete designs.

**6** **Street Market**
MAP N6 ■ Psilinaki, Ierapetra
Every Saturday morning, local farmers and market gardeners set up stalls selling fresh seasonal produce at Ierapetra's street market.

**7** **Si-Mel Savidakis**
MAP Q4 ■ Gela, Sitia ■ www.toplou-honey.com
This place is run by a bee-keeping family. It offers interesting tours and sells its own honey, royal jelly, pollen and *rakomelo* (raki flavoured with honey, to be served hot).

**8** **Domaine Economou**
MAP Q4 ■ Em. Stavrakaki 102, Sitia
Unique Liatiko grapes of the Sitia area are used by Yiannis Economou to produce red wine at this winery (see p79). He learnt his craft in Bordeaux before returning to his native island.

**A range of olive oil at Terra Zakros**

**9** **Terra Zakros**
MAP R5 ■ Ano Zakros ■ www.sitiaterrazakros.gr
This store sells extra-virgin olive oil – awarded silver at the London International Olive Oil Competition 2016 and Athena International Oil Competition 2017 – as well as honey, herbs, wine and *raki* made by local producers.

**10** **Ioannis Petrakis Icons Art Studio**
MAP N4 ■ Mpotis Sfakianakis 8, Elounda ■ www.greek-icons.com
Traditional skills and material are used to create Byzantine and Cretan icons and paintings at this studio (see p79).

*See map on pp110–11* ←

# Bars and Cafés

**1** **Alexandros Rooftop Bar, Agios Nikolaos**
MAP N4 ■ Kondylaki 4

This popular bar serves cocktails at tables with flickering oil lamps and offers romantic views down onto Lake Voulismeni.

**2** **Café-Snack Bar Vaï**

MAP R4 ■ On the beach

In a beautiful setting behind the palm trees on the beach, this café and snack bar offers coffee, drinks, nibbles and ice cream prepared from fresh milk.

**3** **Epico Café Bar, Plaka**

MAP N4 ■ On the beach

Offering fine views of Spinalonga island across the bay, this informal café and wine bar serves chilled beers, freshly squeezed juices, coffee, wine and nibbles.

**4** **Kaaren's, Elounda**
MAP N4 ■ Akti Poseidonos 47
■ 28410 41709

This café-bar *(see p76)* has wonderful views of the sea and serves delicious sandwiches, wraps, homemade sausages and a range of cocktails. Not open for dinner.

Selection of meze at Kaaren's

**5** **Amoodi Club, Agios Nikolaos**

MAP N4 ■ Ammoudi Cove ■ 69733 66065

Combining a fashionable beach bar and sun beds for hire with a slick café-restaurant hosting guest DJs, Ammoudi is a popular waterside summer venue, by day or night.

**Lively night-time scene at Puerto Bar**

**6** **Cafe Puerto Bar, Agios Nikolaos**
MAP N4 ■ Akti Koundourou 9
■ 28410 22850

Enjoy drinks and cocktails at this harbourfront café-bar with great views from its terrace. After dark, retreat indoors as the music begins.

**7** **Ariston Snack and Coffee, Ierapetra**
MAP N6 ■ Stragiou Samouil 14
■ 28420 26120

This modern takeaway offers traditional sticky honey pastries, colourful iced doughnuts, toasted sandwiches, *tyropita* (cheese-filled pies) and other savoury treats.

**8** **Olympio Cafe, Makrygialos**
MAP P5 ■ Makrygialos Harbour
■ 28430 52135

Overlooking the small harbour from under tamarisks, this relaxing café-bar offers full breakfasts, salads, tasty snacks, draught beer and cocktails.

**9** **Mitsakakis, Sitia**
MAP Q4 ■ Karamanli 6

This seafront café is renowned for its homemade Greek desserts, as well as for its excellent ice cream.

**10** **Amnesia, Kato Zakros**
MAP R5 ■ Seafront

All-day beach café-snack bar with a difference – great ice creams, drinks and beers with accompanying nibbles. May get livelier after dark.

# Places to Eat

### 1 Paradosiako, Agios Nikolaos
MAP N4 ▪ Akti Themistokleous 9, Europa Cove ▪ 697 7266 744 ▪ €

A rare find, this is a savoury seaside *mezedopoleio*, where diners tick their choices on the menu or order sheet.

### 2 Kalliotzina, Koutsouras
MAP P5 ▪ Seafront ▪ 28430 51207 ▪ Closed Nov–Apr ▪ €

This taverna *(see p75)* serves good home-cooked meals at outside tables overhung by tamarisk trees.

### 3 Karnagio, Agios Nikolaos
MAP N4 ▪ Kon/nou Paleologou 24 ▪ 2841 025968 ▪ €

Located next to Lake Voulismeni, Karnagio is Agios Nikolaos's most famous restaurant, serving up hearty portions of typical Greek dishes and Cretan cuisine. Book in advance in the high season.

### 4 The Ferryman, Elounda
MAP N4 ▪ Akti Olountos ▪ 28410 41230 ▪ €€

With views across the water to the island of Spinalonga, this seafood taverna *(see p73)* has won many awards. Expect dishes based on fresh local ingredients.

### 5 Akrogiali, Kato Zakros
MAP R5 ▪ On the beach ▪ 28430 26893 ▪ €

A relaxed spot overlooking the beach, Akrogiali serves drinks, seafood and grilled meat.

**Beachside tables at Akrogiali**

### 6 Poulis, Elounda
MAP N4 ▪ Harbourfront ▪ 28410 41451 ▪ Closed Nov–Apr ▪ €€

Poulis *(see p73)* has mainly Cretan and Greek specialities with some international dishes. It also serves a wide selection of grilled seafood, alongside a reasonable wine list.

### 7 Levante, Ierapetra
MAP N6 ▪ Stratigou Samouil 36 ▪ 28420 80585 ▪ €

Next to the Ierapetra beach, Levante is a great place at which to sample regional fare such as *omathies* – sausages stuffed with rice and offal – and *chochlioi bourbouristi* – snails sautéed in lemon and rosemary.

### 8 Piperia, Pefki
MAP Q5 ▪ Eparchiaki Odos Ierapetras ▪ 69367 75069 ▪ €

Soak in the relaxed ambience complemented by the views of the mountainous hinterland and coast, while enjoying the traditional Cretan dishes at this pretty taverna *(see p74)*.

### 9 Ta Kochilia, Mochlos
MAP P4 ▪ Mochlos Seafront ▪ 28430 94432 ▪ €

The oldest (from 1902) local taverna offers seafood, vegetarian platters and daily-changing casseroles, as well as views of Mochlos islet.

### 10 The Balcony, Sitia
MAP Q4 ▪ Foundalidou 19 ▪ 28430 25084 ▪ €€€

Located in an elegant townhouse, this restaurant *(see p72)* serves Cretan cuisine with Asian and Mexican influences. It has an impressive wine list with plenty of local options.

> **PRICE CATEGORIES**
> For a three-course meal for one with half a bottle of wine (or equivalent meal), taxes and extra charges.
> ...........................................................
> € under €25    €€ €25–40    €€€ over €40

See map on pp110–11

# Streetsmart

Vine-filled alleyway in the
Old Town, Chania

# Getting Around

## Arriving by Air

Crete is served by two international airports: **Heraklion** (HER) and **Chania** (CHQ). Heraklion airport lies 5 km (3 miles) east of the and is connected by bus and taxi. It will soon be replaced by a new larger international airport 35 km (22 miles) away from the current one. Chania Airport lies 15 km (9 miles) east of Chania, on the Akrotiri Peninsula; it also has both bus and taxi links. The domestic Sitia Public Airport is located a mere 1.5 km (1 mile) from the city centre, with only taxi or walking access.

From Easter until late October, many international airlines serve Crete. In winter, visitors have to travel to Crete via Athens. There are regular internal flights to either Chania and Heraklion from other Greek islands, including Santorini, Kos and Rhodes.

## Arriving by Sea

Crete has two main ferry ports, Heraklion and Chania, both on the north coast. The port of Heraklion lies opposite the city centre, while Chania's port is at Souda, 7 km (4 miles) east of Chania, to which it is connected by bus.

Daily overnight ferries with comfortable cabins depart from Athens's Piraeus Port for both Heraklion (with a journey time of 9 hours) and Chania (8 hours, 30 minutes). Both routes are jointly operated by **Blue Star Ferries**. In addition, Heraklion and Chania are served by **Minoan Lines**. It is possible to take cars on these ferries.

## Public Transport

Buses are the only form of public transport on Crete. They are run by regional collectives known as Kino Tamio Eispraxeon Leoforon (**KTEL**). Safety and hygiene measures, timetables, ticket information and transport maps can be obtained from the KTEL websites.

## Bus Travel

Frequent, fast KTEL Mercedes buses, usually coloured cream and sea-green, connect the cities of Chania, Rethymno and Heraklion. Some of these buses continue east to Agios Nikolaos. Most of the rest of the island is also served by good bus links, so it is possible to reach most remote villages by public transport. Buses are operated by the **KTEL Chania-Rethymno** and the **KTEL Heraklion and Lasithi** consortia. Tickets need to be bought at kiosks or online before boarding a bus.

## Driving

The main cities along Crete's northern coast – Chania, Heraklion, Agios Nikolaos and Rethymno – are connected by a fast, dual-carriageway motorway known as the Crete National Road (A90).

Due to the nature of the landscape, the road network remains scanty in parts. Roads through the mountainous interior are generally narrow and some are poorly surfaced. In rural areas, you may find livestock on the roads, so caution is advised. Some small villages along the south coast are poorly connected by road – in such cases, it is easier to travel by boat.

During peak season, finding a parking space in the busy towns of Chania, Heraklion and Rethymno can be a problem. It is best to park outside the centre and walk in.

## Car Rental

There are local and international car rental companies at the airports and ferry ports, and in all major towns and resorts. The minimum age for car rental is 21, although some companies require drivers to be over 25. You must have a full, valid driving licence. Driving licences issued by any of the European Union member states are valid; if visiting from outside the EU, you will need to apply for an international driving permit. Opt for a policy insuring you for the collision damage waiver excess beforehand. Renting on the spot is more expensive than booking in advance.

## Rules of the Road

Seatbelts must be worn in front seats, with a €350 fine for non-compliance. Children under 12 must sit in the back seat and under-threes must ride in approved child seats (rental agencies will supply these).

The blood alcohol limit is 0.5 g per litre, and driving under the influence will result in heavy fines, and possible loss of licence and prosecution.

Fines for minor infractions must be paid within ten days to avoid court proceedings. It's an offence to drive away from an accident involving another car – or to move the vehicles from the positions at which they came to rest – before the police arrive, who will breathalyze all drivers and write an accident report. This will be required by your car-hire company and your insurer, even if you are driving your own vehicle.

## Taxis

Taxis on Crete are grey or blue. There are taxi stands near tourist points within the cities, at the airports and ports. You can also hail one in the street. Taxis are inexpensive and operate both in towns and on longer journeys between towns and villages. Short journeys are metered, but for longer trips there is usually a fixed price – agree it before setting off.

## Ferries

The south-coast villages of Paleochora, Sougia, Agia Roumeli, Loutro and Chora Sfakion are connected by boat, but not by road. In summer, ferries operated by **Anendyk** cover this route daily.

**Blue Star Ferries** runs a slow but cheap, twice-a-week service between Heraklion and Rhodes

(journey time 14.5 hours), stopping at Karpathos.

In summer (Apr–Oct), daily high-speed catamarans connect Crete to the Cycladic Islands. Both **Hellenic Seaways** and **SeaJets** run a service from Heraklion to Santorini, Naxos, Paros and Mykonos; SeaJets also sails to Ios. **Fast Ferries** also sails from Heraklion to Santorini, Ios, Paros, Mykonos and Syros, before reaching the port of Piraeus in Athens. The journey from Heraklion to Santorini takes just 2 hours and 30 minutes.

## Cycling

Road cycling on touring or hybrid bikes is common on Crete. Away from the north coast, there are miles of rural roads and farm tracks, ideal for mountain-biking.

Various companies arrange cycling tours and holidays, and bicycles to hire are available in all the main resorts. Cycling is best enjoyed in spring (Apr–May) and autumn (Sep–Oct); mid-summer is feasible only at high altitudes due to the heat.

If you're looking for a challenge, consider taking part in the **Tour of Crete**, a six-day race across the island held each May.

## Walking

The towns of Chania, Rethymno and Heraklion are mostly pedestrian-only and a joy to explore on foot. Some of Crete's most rewarding beaches are quite isolated, and you will have to trek some distance to reach them. Moving into the interior,

Crete offers fantastic landscapes for hiking. The island has several mountains over 2,000 m (6,500 ft), posing a real challenge to hardened walkers and climbers, while its numerous gorges are perfect for novices who prefer easier walking. Organized hiking tours and holidays are very popular.

The E4 European long-distance path *(see p65)* crosses the entire island, running from Kissamos (Kastelli) on the west coast to Kato Zakros on the east.

The best seasons for hiking are spring and autumn.

## DIRECTORY

**ARRIVING BY AIR**
**Chania Airport**
🌐 chq-airport.gr
**Heraklion Airport**
🌐 heraklion-airport.info

**ARRIVING BY SEA**
**Blue Star Ferries**
🌐 bluestarferries.com
**Minoan Lines**
🌐 minoan.gr

**BUS TRAVEL**
**KTEL**
🌐 ktelbus.com
**KTEL Chania–Rethymno**
🌐 e-ktel.com
**KTEL Heraklion and Lasithi**
🌐 ktelherlas.gr

**FERRIES**
**Anendyk**
🌐 anendyk.gr
**Fast Ferries**
🌐 fastferries.com.gr
**Hellenic Seaways**
🌐 hellenicseaways.gr
**SeaJets**
🌐 seajets.gr

**CYCLING**
**Tour of Crete**
🌐 tourofcrete.com

# Practical Information

## Passports and Visas

For entry requirements, including visas, consult your nearest Greek embassy or the **Greek Ministry of Foreign Affairs**. Citizens of the UK, US, Canada, Australia and New Zealand do not need a visa for stays of up to three months but in future must apply in advance for the European Travel Information and Authorization System (**ETIAS**); roll-out has continually been postponed so check website for details. Visitors from other countries may also require an ETIAS, so check before travelling. EU nationals do not need a visa or an ETIAS.

## Government Advice

Now more than ever, it is important to consult both your and the Greek government's advice before travelling. The **UK Foreign, Commonwealth & Development Office**, the **US State Department**, the **Australian Department of Foreign Affairs and Trade** and the **Greek General Secretariat for Civil Protection** offer the latest information on security, health and local regulations.

## Customs Information

You can find information on the laws relating to goods and currency taken in or out of Greece on the **Greek General Directorate of Customs and Excise Duty** website. The unauthorized export of antiquities and art is a serious offence.

## Insurance

We recommend that you take out a comprehensive insurance policy covering theft, loss of belongings, medical care, cancellations and delays, and read the small print carefully. UK citizens are eligible for free emergency medical care in Greece provided they have a valid European Health Insurance Card (EHIC) or UK Global Health Insurance Card (**GHIC**).

## Health

The healthcare system in Greece is made up of a mix of public and private health service providers, and standards can vary depending on your location. Emergency medical care is free for EU and UK nationals at state-run clinics or hospitals, provided you enter via the casualty ward and have a valid EHIC or GHIC. Be sure to present your EHIC or GHIC as soon as possible.

For visitors outside the EU, payment of medical expenses is the patient's responsibility. Organizing comprehensive medical insurance before your trip is essential, as private doctors or clinics can be expensive.

If you require hospital treatment, go to Crete's main hospital, the University General Hospital of Heraklion (PAGNI) on Panepistimiou, which also has a medical school. There are private medical clinics and dentists in all the main towns.

Greek pharmacists can provide comprehensive advice on minor ailments and injuries, and they dispense a wide range of remedies. Most pharmacies, marked by a green cross sign, are open all day Monday to Saturday, and when closed, they have a screen on the door listing nearby duty pharmacies.

Unless otherwise stated, tap water in the Greek Islands is safe to drink, though usually extremely hard. Spring water is avidly collected and the best fountains often have queues.

No inoculations are required to visit Greece.

## Smoking, Alcohol and Drugs

In 2010, Greece introduced a law officially banning smoking in enclosed public spaces, including in restaurants, bars and cafés. Smoking in outdoor areas such as café terraces is usually permitted. Greek police will not tolerate rowdy or indecent behaviour, especially when fuelled by excessive alcohol consumption; Greek courts impose heavy fines or even prison sentences on people who behave indecently. Possession of narcotics is prohibited and could result in a prison sentence.

## ID

Both locals and visitors are required to carry identification (either a national ID cardor passport) on them at all times.

## Personal Security

Crete has a low crime rate but thefts from tourists do sometimes occur. Take sensible precautions with your belongings and never leave anything valuable in the car, even a locked one; the environs of Archaeological Museum of Heraklion's especially are hunting grounds for opportunistic thieves. If you have any thing stolen, you should immediately contact the local **Tourist Police** or go to the police stations in Chania or Heraklion.

The number to call for **general emergencies** is 112. For specific emergencies, call for **Ambulance**, **Police**, **Hospitals** or **SOS Doctors** directly.

As a rule, Greeks are accepting of all people, regardless of their race, gender or sexuality. Homosexuality was legalized in 1951 and civil unions between same-sex couples have been legal since 2015. The influence of the Greek Orthodox church remains strong, however, and in smaller towns and rural areas, which are often more conservative in their views, overt displays of affection may receive frowns from locals. Do not let that discourage you, though. Most Greeks have moved into the 21st century, leaving aside old prejudices.

In Heraklion and other larger towns such as Chania, Rethymon and Agios Nikolaos, there is an LGBTQ+ scene, though it is more discrete than in the Greek Islands' LGBTQ+ capital, Mykonos. A number of LGBTQ+ beaches are scattered around Crete, including Sarantari Beach near Hersonissos, Komos Beach near Matala, Kavros Beach near Georgioupoli and Maherida Beach near Chania.

## Travellers with Specific Requirements

Crete has made some progress in meeting the needs of travellers with accessibility requirements. As of 2018, all hotels must by law provide at least one wheelchair-adapted en-suite room, but compliance will vary. Most modern museums have facilities for people with limited mobility, as do a growing number of beaches. **Disabled Accessible Travel** offers a number of wheelchair accessible tours in Crete.

## Time Zone

Greece is on Eastern European Time (EET), which is two hours ahead of Greenwich Mean Time (GMT) and seven hours ahead of US Eastern Standard Time (EST). Summertime runs from the last Sunday in March to the last Sunday in October.

## DIRECTORY

### PASSPORTS AND VISAS

**ETIAS**
[w] etiasvisa.com

**Greek Ministry of Foreign Affairs**
[w] mfa.gr/en/visas

### GOVERNMENT ADVICE

**Australian Department of Foreign Affairs and Trade**
[w] dfat.gov.au
[w] smartraveller.gov.au

**Greek General Secretariat for Civil Protection**
[w] travel.gov.gr

**UK Foreign, Commonwealth & Development Office**
[w] gov.uk/foreign-travel-advice

**US State Department**
[w] travel.state.gov

### CUSTOMS INFORMATION

**Greek General Directorate of Customs and Excise Duty**
[w] portal.gsis.gr/portal/page/portal/ICISnet

### INSURANCE

**GHIC**
[w] ghic.org.uk

### PERSONAL SECURITY

**Ambulance**
[C] 166
**General Emergencies**
[C] 112
**Hospitals**
[C] 1434
**Police**
[C] 100
**SOS Doctors**
[C] 1016
**Tourist Police**
[C] 171

### TRAVELLERS WITH SPECIFIC REQUIREMENTS

**Disabled Accessible Travel**
[w] disabledaccessibletravel.com

## Money

The currency of Greece is the euro (€). Major credit and debit cards are accepted in most shops and restaurants, while pre-paid currency cards are accepted in some. Contactless cards are widely accepted in large towns – the Greek term for a card machine is *termatiko POS*. However, it is always a good idea to carry some cash as many smaller businesses and markets operate on a cash-only basis, especially those in remote regions of the island. ATMs are widely available in all the major towns and resorts.

It is customary to tip 10 per cent of the total bill at restaurants. Hotel porters and housekeeping will expect a tip of €1–2 per bag or day. For taxi drivers, round up the bill to the next euro.

## Electrical Appliances

The electric current is 230 V (50Hz). Plugs have two round pins. UK visitors will need an adaptor for their appliances, and US visitors may need both a voltage converter and adaptor for their electronic devices.

## Mobile Phones and Wi-Fi

Roaming within the EU for all holders of EU SIMs is free within your monthly call and text allowance. Non-EU visitors should consider buying a local SIM card to save on roaming charges (you will need to have ID). There are three major local providers:

**Cosmote** (with the widest coverage), **NOVA** and **Vodafone**. Most hotels, restaurants and cafés offer free Wi-Fi to guests.

## Postal Services

Greece's **Hellenic Post (ELTA)** has main post offices in **Heraklion**, **Chania** and **Rethymno**, all of them open from 7:30am to 8:30pm Monday to Friday. Post offices in smaller towns and villages close earlier, at 2:30pm. Letter boxes are bright yellow.

## Opening Hours

Cretan opening hours are erratic – use the times given in this book as a rough guide only. Most shops are open from 9am to 2pm Monday to Saturday. On Tuesdays, Thursdays and Fridays, they also open from 5:30 to 8:30pm. In tourist resorts, shops tend to open for longer in summer, sometimes until 10pm.

Banks are open from 8am to 2pm Monday to Thursday and from 8am to 1:30pm Friday.

Major state-run archaeological sites and museums are open from 8am to 8pm in summer; many close on Tuesdays. Last entry is always 20 minutes before closure.

Monasteries, convents and churches are generally open during daylight hours but closed for two to three hours in the afternoon. Banks, businesses and shops are closed on Greek public holidays: New Year's Day (1 Jan), Epiphany (6 Jan), Clean Monday, Independence Day (25 Mar), Good Friday, Easter Sunday, Easter

Monday, Labour Day (1 May), Whit Monday, Assumption (15 Aug), Ohi Day (28 Oct), Christmas (25 Dec) and Boxing Day (26 Dec).

Situations can change quickly and unexpectedly. Always check before visiting attractions and hospitality venues for up-to-date opening hours and booking requirements.

## Weather

Crete has a pleasant Mediterranean climate with plenty of sunshine. Summers are dry, with an average temperature of 26° C (79° F), but frequent maximums of 35° C (95° F). On the coast, gentle sea-breezes make the heat quite bearable.

In winter, the average temperature is 11° C (52° F), but at night it may drop below freezing, and Crete's mountains are often snowcapped from December through to April. Spring and autumn see average temperatures of around 16° C (61° F). Summer (July–August) is the most popular time to visit, but those who prefer milder temperatures, fewer crowds and cheaper rates should consider May–June and September–October.

## Visitor Information

The **Greek National Tourism Organisation (GNTO)** office in Heraklion provides visitors with useful maps, bus time-tables and information about attractions. The

**Region of Crete** website is also full of helpful information.

For general information about the GreekIslands visit the **Greece Is** website. **Odysseus**, the official culture ministry site, gives information, including opening times, for archaeological sites, monuments and state-run museums.

## Language

Greek is the official language. The level of English and other foreign languages spoken can be limited, particularly in rural areas.

## Taxes and Refunds

Usually included in the price, the top rate of FPA (Fóros Prostithémenis Axías) – the equivalent of VAT or sales tax – is 24 per cent in Greece, though taverna meals are taxed at 13 per cent for food. Visitors from outside the EU staying fewer than three months may claim this money back on purchases over €120. A Tax-Free form must be completed in the store, a copy of which is then given to the customs authorities on departure, along with proof of purchase.

## Dining

Cretans tend to eat late: lunch can be any time between 1:30pm and 4pm, while dinner generally starts after 8:30pm and can go on until midnight.

A *taverna* is an informal and inexpensive place serving traditional dishes amid rustic decor. Plates may arrive at the table in a rather haphazard order; this is because there is less definition between courses, and diners often order dishes to share. A *psarotaverna* specializes in fish and seafood.

Other spots include the *mezedopoleio*, serving small platters of *mezedes* (savoury snacks), along with carafes of barrel wine or *raki/tsikoudia*; and the *psistaria*, specializing in spit-roasted and char-grilled meats, especially sausages, chops and spit-roasts. A *gyradiko*, or a *souvlatzidiko* sell the popular *gyros* or *souvlaki* wrapped in pitta bread to take away.

## Accommodation

Crete offers everything from luxury resorts to backpackers' hostels. The biggest concentration of five-star resort hotels, complete with beaches and spas, is in Elounda, near Agios Nikolaos in eastern Crete. Boutique hotels in Chania and Rethymno may occupy Venetian-era buildings with period furnishings. Self-catering apartments offer greater freedom and flexibility. To escape the crowds, opt for a village guesthouse away from the coastal resorts, or to really savour rural life, stay at an agrotourism, a working farm offering accommodation and meals, generally prepared from its own home-grown produce.

Hotel rates depend on supply and demand, and prices peak in high season (Jul–Sep). Room prices almost always include breakfast. Major beachside hotels are closed from November to April. Reliable accommodation sites include **Booking.com** and **The Hotel Guru** for hotels, **HostelWorld** for hostels and budget options, and **Airbnb** for apartments and rooms.

# Places to Stay

PRICE CATEGORIES
For a standard, double room per night (with breakfast if included), taxes and extra charges.

€ under €100  €€ €100–200  €€€ over €200

## Luxury Resorts

### Avra Imperial

MAP C2 ■ Kolymvari ■ 28240 84500 ■ www.avraimperial.gr ■ €€€
Overlooking a sandy beach and a large outdoor pool lined with palms, Avra Imperial is one of western Crete's top resorts. It has 328 rooms and suites (some with private pools), a luxurious spa using Apivita beauty products, and a kids' club.

### Blue Palace Resort and Spa

MAP N4 ■ Plaka, Elounda ■ 28410 65500 ■ www.bluepalace.gr ■ €€€
The Blue Palace offers a superb mix of luxury suites, bungalows and villas with a spa, health centre, indoor and outdoor pools and tennis courts, plus a range of watersports.

### Creta Maris Beach Resort

MAP M4 ■ Hersonissos ■ 28970 27000 ■ www.metaxahospitality.gr ■ €€€
Located on the beach, the Creta Maris aims to provide a village atmosphere, with paths winding through lush grounds past a mix of bungalows, suites and rooms. The resort also offers a luxurious spa and activities such as Cretan dancing and cooking.

### Daios Cove Luxury Resort

MAP N4 ■ Vathi, Agios Nikolaos ■ 28418 88019 ■ www.daioscovecrete.com ■ €€€
All rooms and suites have sea views at this family-friendly resort, and the villas have private pools. There is a beach offering watersports, tennis courts, a spa and a kids' club.

### Domes of Elounda

MAP N4 ■ Elounda ■ 28410 43500 ■ www.domesresorts.com ■ €€€
Renowned for luxury and top service, this resort caters for both couples and families, with adult-only areas and a kids' club. It offers suites, residences and villas, a beach, a spa and four restaurants.

### Elounda Mare Hotel, Relais and Chateau

MAP N4 ■ S of Elounda ■ 28410 68200 ■ www.eloundamare.com ■ €€€
The 96 units here include a mix of standard doubles and bungalows and suites with private pools. Facilities include a nine-hole golf course, a spa and watersports.

### Elounda Peninsula

MAP N4 ■ S of Elounda ■ 28410 68250 ■ www.eloundapeninsula.com ■ €€€
On its own private peninsula, this hotel has duplex suites, as well as larger villas with private pools. Facilities include a spa, tennis courts and a kids' club.

### Grecotel Creta Palace

MAP F3 ■ Misiria ■ 28310 55181 ■ www.creta palace.com ■ €€€
Close to Rethymno, Creta Palace has 162 rooms in its main block, plus 200 bungalows and villas. It has several pools and a wide range of activities for children, as well as tennis courts and watersports.

### Minoa Palace Resort & Spa

MAP C2 ■ Agia Marina ■ 28210 36500 ■ www.minoapalace.gr ■ €€€
Close to Platanias and Chania, the Minoa Palace has a variety of rooms, suites and bungalows, some with private pools.

### Minos Beach Art Hotel

MAP N4 ■ Agios Nikolaos ■ 28410 22345 ■ www.minosbeach.com ■ €€€
This medium-sized complex of bungalows is set in tranquil gardens with views of the Gulf of Mirabello. A short stroll from the town centre, the hotel has its own sandy beaches and rocky inlets.

### Out of the Blue Resort and Spa

MAP K3 ■ Agia Pelagia, Heraklion ■ 28108 11112 ■ www.capsis.com ■ €€€
On a private headland, this five-star resort has its own beaches, a huge swimming pool, a kids' club, restaurants and bars. Ideal for groups or families looking to stay in exclusive villas.

### St Nicolas Bay Resort
MAP N4 ▪ Nisi Peninsula ▪ 28410 90200 ▪ www.stnicolasbay.gr ▪ €€€
This multi award-winning complex, just outside Agios Nikolaos, has well-equipped rooms, suites and villas, and three restaurants. Watersports are also offered.

### Galaxy Hotel Heraklion
MAP U3 ▪ Dimokratias 75 ▪ 2810238812 ▪ €€
One of the few hotels in town with a swimming pool, this five-star luxury site also features a gym, two fine restaurants and a brilliant breakfast service. Its location close to the port and Heraklion's centre cannot be beaten.

## Boutique Hotels

### Alcanea Boutique Hotel
MAP A5 ▪ Angelou 2, Chania ▪ 28210 75370 ▪ Closed in winter ▪ www.ariahotels.gr ▪ €€
Situated in the harbour, above the Naval Museum, this hotel occupies the former office of Cretan revolutionary statesman Elef-therios Venizelos. Rooms are painted in soothing pastels and have views of the harbour and sea.

### Avli Lounge Suites
MAP Q2 ▪ Rethymno ▪ 28310 58250 ▪ Open all year ▪ www.avli.gr ▪ €€
Centrally located, Avli has 12 suites, some with a Jacuzzi or terrace, spread over three Venetian-era buildings. Breakfast is served in the courtyard restaurant, along with a less formal *mezedopoleio*, Raki Ba Raki.

### Casa Vitae Villas
MAP Q2 ▪ Neophytou Patelarou 3, Rethymno ▪ 28310 35058 ▪ www.casa-vitae.gr ▪ €€
In a Venetian-era building with a courtyard (where breakfast is served), these doubles or suites have exposed stone walls, tiled floors and wooden-beamed ceilings. Some rooms also have a four-poster bed, a balcony or a Jacuzzi bath.

### Mythos Suites Hotel
MAP F3 ▪ C12 Plateia Karaoli, Rethymno ▪ 28310 53917 ▪ www.mythoshotelsuites.com ▪ €€
This hotel occupies two 16th-century Venetian buildings that have been knocked together. It is centred on a courtyard with a pool; ground floor rooms have verandas, while rooms on the upper floors have wooden balconies.

### Palazzino di Corina
MAP Q1 ▪ Damvergi 7–9, Rethymno ▪ 28310 21205/06 ▪ www.corina.gr ▪ €€
This lovingly restored Venetian mansion in the old town has 29 small rooms and suites, some with Jacuzzi baths and four-poster beds. There is a plunge-pool in the charming patio, a lively street-side bar and an excellent restaurant.

### Pandora Suites
MAP D2 ▪ Lithinon 29, Chania ▪ 28210 43588 ▪ www.pandorasuites.com ▪ €€
This is a stylish collection of two- and four-person suites, some facing an inner courtyard, others looking out to sea. All have balconies and tall, shuttered windows. With views of the old Venetian port and the lighthouse, guests can enjoy their breakfast or have a drink at the hotel's roof garden.

### Ambassador Residence Boutique Hotel
MAP D2 ▪ Akti Tompazi 29–30, Chania ▪ 28216 00855 ▪ www.ambassadorsresidence chania.com ▪ €€€
In a 19th-century building overlooking the harbour, these nine suites are contemporary and stylish. Each is inspired by a different material: wood, ceramic or glass. Some have a terrace or a Jacuzzi.

### Casa Delfino
MAP D2 ▪ Theofanous 9, Chania ▪ 28210 93098 ▪ www.casadelfino.com ▪ €€€
This early 17th-century, Venetian-built mansion, Chania's most exclusive address, has been luxuriously restored by a descendant of the original Delfino family. All 24 suites are unique, having a *hamam* or vaulted ceiling, balcony or even a roof terrace. The hotel also features a gift shop as well as a bijou spa.

### Casa Leone Hotel
MAP D2 ▪ Parodos Theotokopolou 18, Chania ▪ 28210 75370 ▪ www.casa-leone.com ▪ €€€
The "House of the Lion" has been meticulously restored, with period details such as Venetian mirrors and antique and reproduction furniture.

## Kapsaliana Village Hotel

MAP G4 ■ Kapsaliana, near Arkadi ■ 28310 83400 ■ www.kapsaliana village.gr ■ €€€

Twelve typically Cretan and Venetian houses in this village have been converted into 17 guesthouses, each combining original features with modern comforts such as Wi-Fi and DVD players. The complex also has a pool, a restaurant and an old olive press.

## La Maison Ottomane

MAP A5 ■ Parodos Kanevarou 32, Chania ■ 28210 08796 ■ www. lamaisonottomane.com ■ €€€

This romantic hideaway has just three elegant rooms, furnished with period antiques and artworks, plus modern luxuries such as in-room espresso machines and tablet computers. Breakfast and drinks are served in a pretty, peaceful courtyard.

## Villa Andromeda

MAP D2 ■ Elfetheriou Venizelou 150, Chania ■ 28210 28300 ■ Closed Nov–Mar ■ www.villand romeda.gr ■ €€€

This converted Neo-Classical mansion has eight wood-floored suites, many with balconies, painted ceilings in the communal areas and a landscaped pool.

## Beach Hotels

### Alianthos Garden Hotel

MAP F4 ■ Plakias ■ 28320 31280 ■ www.hotel alianthos.com ■ €€

A block inland from one of Crete's nicest beaches, this family-run hotel is the best in Plakias. It has a children's pool, freshwater pool and poolside bar, plus a market and a restaurant.

## Ammos Hotel

MAP C2 ■ Agioi Apostoli ■ 28210 33003 ■ www. ammoshotel.com ■ Closed Dec–Mar ■ €€

Behind a sandy beach, this stylish hotel west of Chania is filled with hip design and artworks. It has 33 mostly sea-view studios or suites, plus an all-day restaurant, pool, massage room, gym and playroom.

## Corinna Mare

MAP D2 ■ Kalamaki, Nea Kydonia ■ 28210 31767 ■ www.corinna.gr ■ €€

On a small peninsula west of Chania, facing Theo-dorou islet, this peaceful hotel has 49 rooms, suites and apartments. There is a restaurant, two outdoor pools, sauna and gym, plus baby-sitting and massage on request.

## Iberostar Creta Panorama & Mare

MAP G3 ■ Panormos ■ 28340 51502 ■ www. iberostar.com ■ €€

Four outdoor pools, a heated indoor pool, six tennis courts, sauna and water sports, make this huge beach resort one of the best in Crete for an active holiday. Accommodation is in suites or bungalows.

## Irini Mare

MAP G5 ■ Main beach, Agia Galini ■ 28320 91051 ■ www.irinimare. com ■ €€

This is a small, family-run hotel in a tranquil spot. There is a pool and a kids' playground, and most rooms or suites have balconies with a sea view. Great buffet breakfasts and half-board rates.

## Kalyves Beach Hotel

MAP E2 ■ Kalyves ■ 28250 31285 ■ www. kalyvesbeach.com ■ €€

Situated between two sandy beaches on Souda Bay, this hotel overlooks the Xydas river and has 150 rooms in two wings, each with a pool. There is an attractive riverside terrace restaurant and easy beach access.

## Porto Loutro Hotel

MAP D4 ■ Loutro, Anopoli ■ 28250 91433 ■ No credit cards ■ www. hotelportoloutro.com ■ €€

This attractive hotel just above the shoreline has 36 rooms (plus four self-catering studios) in two buildings in separate parts of this village, set among palm trees and bougainvillea. No children under seven are allowed.

## Sitia Bay Hotel

MAP Q4 ■ Patriarhou Vartholomeou 27/Tritis Septemvriou 8, Sitia ■ 28430 24800 ■ www. sitiabay.com ■ €€

This hotel has 19 studios and suites with kitchens and balconies with sea views. Amenities include free Wi-Fi and a rooftop terrace. There is also a small gym, a sauna and a chlorine-free pool with hydro-massage.

## Pilot Beach Resort

MAP E3 ■ Georgioupoli ■ 28250 61901 ■ www. pilot-beach.gr ■ €€€

This resort has well-appointed bungalows and suites, extensive sports facilities, pools and plenty of fun activities for kids. Enjoy food and nightlife in the resort's four restau-rants and three bars.

## Village Guesthouses

### Aspros Potamos Cottages

MAP P5 ■ Aspros Potamos, Makrygialos, Ierapetra ■ 28430 51694 ■ No air conditioning ■ www. asprospotamos.com ■ €

These utterly lovely shepherds' cottages, with stone floors, wooden ceilings and fireplace nooks, are set among groves of pine, olive and carob trees. Although accommodation is self-catering, breakfast is available on request. There is a tiny swimming pool on site.

### The Blue House

MAP D4 ■ Loutro ■ 28250 91035 ■ €

Balconies overlook the bay and the slopes of the White Mountains at this amiable guesthouse. It is particularly handy as an overnight stop on the way to or from Agia Roumeli and the Samaria Gorge.

### Corali Studios and Portobello Apartments

MAP N4 ■ Akti Posidonos, Elounda ■ 28410 41712 ■ www.coralistudios.com ■ €

A short walk from the town centre, these family-run studios and apart-ments have their own pool and gardens. They also offer easy access to the town beach and watersports.

### Hotel Marina

MAP H4 ■ Main street, Anogeia ■ 28340 31817 ■ €

This modern village inn has 16 apartments, including four larger ones for families. Each apart-ment has a kitchen, a TV, a balcony with a view of the Psiloritis range and a fireplace.

### Keramos Studios

MAP J5 ■ Zaros ■ 69705 79395 ■ www.studio keramos-zaros.gr ■ €

Famous for its breakfasts, which include home-made pies and cheeses, this welcoming, family-run B&B offers 18 basic but comfortable rooms with balconies, a lounge with a fireplace, and visits to the family farm.

### Terramara Rooms

MAP B2 ■ Plakalona, Kissamos ■ 69406 94904 ■ No credit cards ■ www. terramaracrete.com ■ €

On a hill surrounded by olive groves, Terramara offers spectacular views of the Gulf of Kissamos. Facilities include a pool, barbecue area, bar and laundry service. There are four inter-connected rooms that are ideal for families.

### Arolithos

MAP J4 ■ Arolithos, Servili, Tylissos ■ 2810 821050 ■ www.arolithos.com ■ €€

At this complex of stone houses, you can take part in an array of tradi-tional crafts – from pottery and icon painting, to basket weaving and embroidery. Traditional music and dance are performed nightly in the affiliated restaurant.

### Koutsounari Traditional Cottages

MAP N6 ■ Koutsounari, 9 km (6 miles) from Ierapetra ■ 28420 61815 ■ Some air conditioning ■ www.tradi tionalcottages.gr ■ €€

Stay in a fully modernized stone cottage or studio at this hillside holiday village. All have verandas or gardens, and there is a pool and taverna next door. Minimum stay is a week.

### Monastery Estate Guesthouse

MAP C4 ■ 4 km above Moni, Sougia ■ 28230 51344 ■ www.monastery estate.com ■ €€

In the mountains near Sougia, this complex of 19th-century buildings has been turned into five luxu-rious two-room apart-ments. Each has a kitchen and terrace.

### Rodanthi Guesthouse

MAP E3 ■ Kastellos, Apokoronas ■ 28210 58500 ■ www.rodanthi hotel.gr ■ €€

In a beautiful hillside village between Chania and Rethymno, this farmhouse stands in a walled garden with a large pool and barbecue. Its four rooms have period furniture, and there is a kitchen where guests can make their own breakfast.

### Villa Archanes

MAP K4 ■ Ano Archanes ■ 69724 43466 ■ www. villaarchanes.gr ■ €€

Providing a fine base for winery visits, this stone mansion from 1890 lies in vineyard country, south of Heraklion. It has six apart-ments (sleeping two–five), an outdoor pool and bar-becue, and a gym, plus massage on request.

*For a key to hotel price categories see p128*

### Villa Kerasia
MAP J4 ■ Vlachiana
■ 2810 791021 ■ www.
villa-kerasia.gr ■ €€
Some 15 km (9 miles)
inland from Heraklion,
with hiking trails nearby,
this welcoming villa is set
in a garden with a pool. It
offers seven rooms, some
with four-poster beds.

## Self-Catering Apartments

### AnnaView Apartments
MAP F4 ■ Myrthios village
■ 697 3324 775 ■ Open
all year ■ www.annaview.
com ■ €
Constructed in wood and
stone, these family-run
apartments have spectac-
ular views over Plakias Bay.
Beautifully furnished, they
come with a kitchenette,
satellite TV and Wi-Fi.

### BayView Apartments
MAP Q4 ■ Petras, Sitia
■ 28430 24333 ■ No credit
cards ■ No air conditioning
■ Winter rentals by the
month ■ www.bayview-
apartments.gr ■ €
Located near the main
Sitia beach, these seven
apartments (three one-bedroom, four two-bedrooms)
have pleasant furnishings
and superb views over
the bay and the town.

### Lefka Apartments
MAP D2 ■ Odos Omirou,
Chania ■ 28210 73310
■ www.lefka-apartments.
gr ■ €
Just outside Chania, close
to some lovely beaches,
the Lefka apartment
complex has a garden
with a free-form pool
and snack bar. The eight
studios and eight apart-
ments (sleeping two–four)
are basic but come with
kitchens and balconies.

### Metohi Vaï Village
MAP R4 ■ S of Vaï Beach
■ 28430 61071 ■ www.4ty.
gr/merchant/12313/en/
METOCHIVAI ■ €
The only accommodation
option this close to the
Vaï palm beach. The
seven apartments here
occupy old shepherds'
shelters converted into
comfortable apartments
with kitchens and soaring
arches. Some have
working fireplaces.

### Paul Eva Apartments
MAP M4 ■ Sokratous 15,
Koutouloufari, Hersonissos
■ 28970 23358 ■ €
Extremely affordable
apartments, only 1 km
(half a mile) from the
beach, each with private
balconies and basic ame-
nities, plus a shared pool.

### Stella's Traditional Apartments
MAP R5 ■ Kato Zakros
village ■ 28430 23739
■ www.stelapts.com ■ €
Stella's offers stone-built,
traditionally furnished
studios (fits 2–4) or larger
apartments in the Terra
Minoika section, set
amid lush landscaping
with hammocks on the
terrace. There is fresh
spring water on tap, and
a communal clothes
washing machine.

### Villa Anna
MAP B4 ■ Paleochora
■ 2810 346428 ■ No credit
cards ■ www.villaanna-
paleochora.com ■ €
Set amid vast gardens,
this 8-unit complex is
located on a quiet side
street close to the sandy
beach. All apartments
have a living room, kitchen
and veranda, plus one or
two bedrooms. There is
also a children's play area.

### Aptera Hotel
MAP D2 ■ Aptera,
Apokoronou, Chania
■ 69793 91308 ■ No credit
cards ■ Breakfast available
on extra charge ■ www.
aptera-lodge.com ■ €€
These well-equipped studio
and one or two bedroom
apartments near the ancient
Aptera overlook Souda Bay
and the White Mountains.

### Elounda Water Park Residence
MAP N4 ■ Odos
Emmanouil Pouli, Schisma,
Elounda ■ 28410 41823
■ www.eloundaresidence.
gr ■ €€
Set in lush gardens a
15-minute walk south of
central Elounda, this complex has a water park and
an all-inclusive meal plan
that complements its few
villas and apartments.
Other facilities include
a saltwater pool, a kids'
club and a gym.

### Natalia's Houses
MAP E3 ■ Douliana village
■ 28250 23356 ■ www.
nataliashouses.gr ■ €€
Charming Natalia's has
four self-catering suites
(two with fireplaces) in
restored stone buildings,
which can accommodate
three to six people. There
is a shop, a pool, a bar
and a barbecue area.
Guests can enjoy views
of the White Mountains
from here.

### White River Cottages
MAP P5 ■ Aspros Potamos,
Makrygialos ■ 28430
51120 ■ www.white
rivercottages.com ■ €€
This romantic boho-chic
retreat surrounded by
olive groves comprises
15 self-catering cottages
(capacity two–four) built
into the rock, with stone

floors and wooden ceilings. The large, deep focal pool has gazebos for shade and reliable Wi-Fi signal.

### Yiannis Retreat

MAP R5 ■ Kato Zakros, 500 m (1,640 ft) inland ■ 28430 25726 ■ www. katozakros-rooms.gr ■ €€

In a lush garden with palms, hammocks and a barbecue area, these five studios have exposed stone walls, terracotta floors, wooden-beamed ceilings, traditional wooden furniture and kitchenettes. Mountain bikes are available for free.

## Agrotourism

### Argoulias

MAP M4 ■ Tzermiado ■ 69722 34275 ■ www. argoulias.gr ■ €

Comprising 11 stone-built apartments and a rustic restaurant serving breakfast, Argoulias also arranges hiking trips and local farm visits on the Lasithi Plateau.

### Ktima Orgon

MAP L4 ■ Apostoli ■ 69748 91750 ■ www. orgonfarm.gr ■ €

Set amid olive groves, around 35 minutes' drive from Heraklion, this self-catering family cottage on an organic olive farm sleeps up to six people. Guests can also learn how to make local products such as grape molasses, wine, *raki* and olive oil-based soaps and salves.

### Lasinthos Eco Park

MAP M5 ■ Agios Georgios ■ 28440 89101 ■ www.lasinthos.gr ■ €

On the Lasithi Plateau, this eco-park has 20 apart-

ments and a restaurant. It is ideal for families with children. Activities on offer include craft workshops and feeding the animals – goats, sheep, cows, horses, chickens and ducks.

### Milia Mountain Retreat

MAP B3 ■ Milia, Vlatos ■ 28210 46774 ■ www. staging7.milia.gr ■ €

Set in a wooded valley, accessed via a winding rough track, Milia offers 13 rooms in restored stone cottages, heated by wood-burning stoves, with mountain spring water and solar-panel electricity. The retreat's taverna serves several local delicacies.

### Mourtzanakis Residence

MAP K3 ■ Achlada ■ 2810 812096 ■ www. ecotourismgreece.com ■ €

In the hills behind Agia Pelagia, this welcoming ecotourism centre offers modern purpose-built apartments, two small pools (kids/adults) and optional communal meals. It also offers a special "olive harvest" package.

### Thalori Traditional Ecotourism Village

MAP K6 ■ Kapetaniana ■ 28930 41762 ■ www. thalori.com ■ €

In the mountains above the south coast, this rural retreat offers 20 studios and cottages with exposed stone walls and wooden-beamed ceilings, as well as a taverna that uses local produce. Thalori makes a fine base for hiking and visiting nearby beaches.

### Dalabelos

MAP G3 ■ Angeliana ■ 28340 22155 ■ www. dalabelos.gr ■ €€

With vineyards and orchards, this farm has ten stone-built one-bedroom apartments, a courtyard restaurant with its own wine, and a pool. Guests are welcome to help on the farm.

### Eleonas Country Village

MAP H5 ■ Zaros ■ 28940 31238 ■ www.eleonas.gr ■ €€

A farm with olive groves, Eleonas has 20 stone cottages, an outdoor pool, bikes for hire and an excellent taverna (see p97) that serves dishes made from local produce. It is set in a lovely rural location, with a gorge and a lake accessible via marked hiking paths.

### Enagron

MAP H4 ■ Axos Mylopotamou ■ 28340 61611 ■ www.enagron.gr ■ €€

Located amid lush vineyards and olive groves, this ecotourism complex has 32 purpose-built, stone-and-wood apartments (studios–three rooms), a taverna, a café, a spa and an outdoor pool. Activities include bread-making and wine tasting.

### Vamos Traditional Guesthouses

MAP E3 ■ Vamos, Apokoronas ■ 28250 22190 ■ www.vamos village.gr ■ €€

In an abandoned former village, these stone villas and cottages have been lovingly restored; family-sized ones also have pools. Vamos arranges cookery lessons, olive-mill and winery visits, and hiking.

*For a key to hotel price categories see p128*

# General Index

# Acknowledgments

## This edition updated by

**Contributor** Gabi Ancarola
**Senior Editors** Dipika Dasgupta, Zoë Rutland
**Senior Art Editor** Vinita Venugopal
**Project Editor** Lucy Sara Kelly
**Assistant Art Editor** Bineet Kaur
**Assistant Editor** Abhidha Lakhera
**Assistant Picture Research Administrator**
Manpreet Kaur
**Project Picture Researcher** Nishwan Rasool
**Publishing Assistant** Simona Velikova
**Jacket Picture Researcher** Jordan Lambley
**Jacket Designer** Divyanshi Shreyaskar
**Senior Cartographer** Subhashree Bharati
**Cartography Manager** Suresh Kumar
**Senior DTP Designer** Tanveer Zaidi
**Senior Production Editor** Jason Little
**Senior Production Controller** Samantha Cross
**Managing Editors** Shikha Kulkarni,
Beverly Smart, Hollie Teague
**Senior Managing Art Editor** Priyanka Thakur
**Art Director** Maxine Pedliham
**Publishing Director** Georgina Dee

DK would like to thank the following for their
contribution to the previous editions:
Robin Gauldie, Jane Foster, Laura Walker,
Helen Peters

The publisher would like to thank the
following for their kind permission to
reproduce their photographs:

**Key:** a-above; b-below/bottom; c-centre;
f-far; l-left; r-right; t-top

**123RF.com:** Guillermo Avello 98–9; dziewul
4cl, 26-7, 44tl; freeartist 115b; Olga Gavrilova
3tr, 120-1; Patryk Kośmider 16–7.

**4Corners:** Reinhard Schmid 20–1, 79cl, SIME
/Johanna Huber 101tl, /Ugo Mellone 64b, /
Riccardo Spila 7t, 61tr, 115cr.

**Abea Deli:** 107br.

**Alamy Stock Photo:** AegeanPhoto 10cla;
age fotostock 67bl; ART Collection 52b; dpa
picture alliance archive 67tr; Peter Eastland
63br; Peter Forsberg 16cl; Hackenberg-
Photo-Cologne 18cr, 45br, 48b, 51cl,
68tl, 72bl, 74–5, 75cl, 76t, 77clb, 80tr,
84tl, 91cla, 112tr; Hemis 60cr; Peter Horree
52tl; ImageBROKER 50tl, 55bl; IML Image
Group Ltd 73tr; INTERFOTO 40bl; Joana
Kruse 88ca; Tony Lilley 12cl; Hercules Milas
2tr, 4crb, 6tr,
13clb, 17tl, 19br, 24cr, 31tl, 32clb, 32–3,
33bl, 38–9, 41tl, 56b, 65cla, 70bl; Pacific
Press 56tl; Anthony Palmer 71tl; Photo 12
53tl; PjrTravel 21tl, 52c; Tim Rainey 118tr;
Stefano Ravera 83clb; SagaPhoto.Com /
Forget Patrick 45cl; Marco Simoni 10c;

Charles Stirling (Travel) 57cl; TravelCollection
82t; Georgios Tsichlis 13cr; Tony Watson
26br; Zoonar GmbH 63cl.

**Athos Workshop:** 107c.

**Avli:** 72t, 109bl.

**AWL Images:** Walter Bibikow 28–9; Christian
Heeb 28crb; ImageBROKER 29crb, 114clb;
Katja Kreder 61b, 69cl; Doug Pearson 29br.

**Depositphotos Inc:** Arsty 100tl; juliane33
11ca.

**Dreamstime.com:** 88and84 83tr; Rostislav
Ageev 15bl; Alp Aksoy 70tl; Alexxich 47b;
Anilah 22, 111br; Arenaphotouk 11crb, 36–7;
Arsty 2tl, 8-9, 10b, 17cl, 43tr; Artcasta 58-9;
Asafta 43c; Mila Atkovska 4b, 6cl, 36bl;
Banepetkovic 12-3; Ccat82 37crb; Anton
Chygarev 111tl; Chasdesign1983 1; Dbyjuhfl
11bl; Dudlajzov 90c; Dziewul 4cla, 11tr, 11cra,
30cla, 64tl, 81cl, 102cla; Ej Rodriquez
Photography 34cl, 35bl; Inna Felker 74tr, 75tr;
Evgeniy Fesenko 27br; Flavijus 105cla;
H368k742 4cra; Bensliman Hassan 27tl;
Gabriela Insuratelu 11clb, 55tl; Gorelovs 108t;
Panagiotis Karapanagiotis 4clb, 29tl, 31crb,
65br; Pavel Kavalenkau 20cl; Denis Kelly
10cra; Kokixx 85cla; Patryk Kosmider 84–5,
110cla; Sergii Koval 77tr; Ksya 51tr; Lornet
94tl; Lucianbolca 18b, 93b; Artur Maltsau
12br; Miradrozdowski 92cla; Mirc3a 102-3;
Mnf1974 62cl; Naturefriend 66bc; Nomadbeg
18tl; Alessio Orrù 71cl; Anna Pakutina 14t,
19tl, 19c, 48c; Marek Poplawski 58tl;
Singidavar 3tl; Maria Sokor 76br; Smallredgirl
85tr; Theripper 67cla; Tupungato 21cl;
Tuulijumala 43b; Vitmark 47cra; David
Watmough 37tl; Xiaoma 40t, 71br, 90tl;
Zaramira 33tl, 89tr.

**Eleaons, Zaros:** 97cr.

**Flakatoras Ceramics:** 106tl.

**Getty Images:** DEA /Archivio J. Lange
24cl, 27c, 49c, 53br; De Agostini / Archivio.
Lange 42clb; Dosfotos / Design Pics 78b;
Hulton Archive / Keystone 41clb; Bastian
Parschau 81br; / Print Collector 454t; Javier
Fernández Sánchez 66clb; Universal History
Archive 14clb; UniversalImagesGroup 41tr.

**Getty Images/iStock:** fotokon 63t;
FrankvandenBergh 114tr; gionnixxx 25crb;
Gatsi 34-35c; jlazouphoto 35tr; Vladimirs_
Gorelovs 116b; lucianbolca 80b;
PanosKarapanagiotis 4t; PaulCowan 25tl;
Saro17 30bl; stamkar 69br; VladimirSklyarov
68b, 112–3.

**Kaaren's, Elounda:** 118crb.

**Municipality of Chania:** 49cla.

**Nikos Siragas:** 79br.

**Ourios Ceramics:** 106c.

**Shutterstock.com:** Stefanos Rapanis /EPA 82clb; T photography 57tr; Georgios Tsichlis 104b.

**Robert Harding Picture Library:** Stuart Black 15cr; Maria Breuer 59cra.

**Scalani Hills Boutari Winery & Residences:** 95cl.

**Terra Zakros:** 117cr.

**SuperStock:** age fotostock /Peter Erik Forsberg 96t, /Phil Robinson 78tl; Albatross 46clb; Album /Oronoz 54c; BEW Authors / BE&W 44b; Katja Kreder / imageBROKER 119bl; Juniors 66tl.

**Veneto, Rethymno:** 73clb.

### Cover

Front and spine: **Dreamstime.com:** Chasdesign1983

Back: **Alamy Stock Photo:** imageBROKER tl, Jan Wlodarczyk cla;
**Dreamstime.com:** Chasdesign1983 b.
**Getty Images/iStock:** Anna_Jedynak crb;
**Robert Harding Picture Library:** Neil Farrin tr.

### Pull Out Map Cover

**Dreamstime.com:** Chasdesign1983

All other images © Dorling Kindersley

For further information see:
www.dkimages.com

**Commissioned Photography** Robin Gauldie, Rough Guides / Geoff Garvey, Tony Souter

**DK** | Penguin Random House

First Edition 2003

First Published in Great Britain by
Dorling Kindersley Limited,
One Embassy Gardens, 8 Viaduct
Gardens, London, SW11 7BW, UK

The authorised representative in the EEA is
Dorling Kindersley Verlag GmbH.
Arnulfstr.124, 80636 Munich, Germany

Published in the United States by
DK Publishing, 1745 Broadway, 20th Floor,
New York, NY 10019, USA

Copyright © 2003, 2024 Dorling
Kindersley Limited

A Penguin Random House Company

24 25 26 27 10 9 8 7 6 5 4 3 2 1

All rights reserved. No part of this
publication may be reproduced, stored in
or introduced into a retrieval system, or
transmitted in any form, or by any means
(electronic, mechanical, photocopying,
recording or otherwise) without the prior
written permission of the copyright owner.

The publishers cannot accept responsibility
for any consequences arising from the use
of this book, nor for any material on third
party websites, and cannot guarantee that
any website address in this book will be a
suitable source of travel information.

A CIP catalogue record is available
from the British Library.

A catalogue record for this book is available
from the Library of Congress.

ISSN 1479-344X

ISBN 978-0-2416-6964-8

Printed and bound in Malaysia

www.dk.com

*As a guide to abbreviations in visitor information
blocks:* **Adm** = admission charge; **D** = dinner.

**MIX**
Paper | Supporting
responsible forestry
**FSC™ C018179**
www.fsc.org

This book was made with Forest
Stewardship Council™ certified
paper – one small step in DK's
commitment to a sustainable future.
Learn more at **www.dk.com/uk/
information/sustainability**

# Phrase Book

## In an Emergency

| | | |
|---|---|---|
| Help! | Voítheia! | vo-ee-theea! |
| Stop! | Stamatíste! | sta-ma-tee-steh! |
| Call a doctor! | Fonáxte éna giatró! | fo-nak-steh e-na ya-tro! |
| Call an ambulance! | Kaléste to asthenofóro/tin | ka-le-steh to as-the-no-fo-ro/teen |
| the police/fire brigade! | astynomía/tin pyrosvestiki! | a-sti-no-the mía/teen pee-ro-zve-stee-kee! |
| Where is the nearest telephone/hospital/pharmacy? | Poú eínai to plisiéstero tiléfono/nosokomeío/farmakeío? | poo ee-ne to plee-see-e-ste-ro tee-le-pho-no/no-so-ko-mee-o/far-ma-kee-o? |

## Communication Essentials

| | | |
|---|---|---|
| Yes | Nai | neh |
| No | Ochi | o-chee |
| Please | Parakaló | pa-ra-ka-lo |
| Thank you | Efcharistó | ef-cha-ree-sto |
| You are welcome | Parakaló | pa-ra-ka-lo |
| OK/alright | Entáxei | en-dak-zee |
| Excuse me | Me synchoreíte | me seen-cho-ree-teh |
| Hello | Geiá sas | yeea sas |
| Goodbye | Antío | an-dee-o |
| Good morning | Kaliméra | ka-lee-me-ra |
| Good night | Kalin'ychta | ka-lee-neech-ta |
| Morning | Proí | pro-ee |
| Afternoon | Apógevma | a-po-yev-ma |
| Evening | Vrádi | vrath-i |
| This morning | Símera to proí | see-me-ra to pro-ee |
| Yesterday | Chthés | chthes |
| Today | Símera | see-me-ra |
| Tomorrow | Avrio | av-ree-o |
| Here | Edó | ed-o |
| There | Ekeí | e-kee |
| What? | Tí? | tee? |
| Why? | Giatí? | ya-tee? |
| Where? | Poú? | poo? |
| How? | Pós? | pos? |
| Wait! | Perímene! | pe-ree-me-neh! |
| How are you? | Tí káneis? | tee ka-nees? |
| Very well, thank you. | Polý kalá, efcharistó. | po-lee ka-la, ef-cha-ree-sto. |
| How do you do? | Pós eíste? | pos ees-te? |
| Pleased to meet you. | Chaíro pol'y. | che-ro po-lee. |
| What is your name? | Pós légeste? | pos le-ye-ste? |
| Where is/are…? | Poú eínai…? | poo ee-neá? |
| How far is it to…? | Póso apéchei…? | po-so a-pe-chee? |
| How do I get to..? | Pós mporó na páo…? | pos bo-ro-na pa-o…? |
| Do you speak English? | Miláte Angliká? | mee-la-te an-glee-ka? |
| I understand. | Katalavaíno. | ka-ta-la-ve-no. |
| I don't understand | Den katalavaíno. | then ka-ta-la-ve-no. |
| Could you speak slowly? | Miláte lígo pio argá parakaló? | mee-la-te lee-go pyo ar-ga pa-ra-ka-lo? |
| I'm sorry. | Me synchoreíte. | me seen-cho-ree teh. |
| Does anyone have a key? | Echei kanénas kleidí? | e-chee ka-ne-nas klee-dee? |

## Useful Words

| | | |
|---|---|---|
| big | Megálo | me-ga-lo |
| small | Mikró | mi-kro |
| hot | Zestó | zes-to |
| cold | Kr'yo | kree-o |
| good | Kaló | ka-lo |
| bad | Kakó | ka-ko |
| enough | Arketá | ar-ke-ta |

| | | |
|---|---|---|
| well | Kalá | ka-la |
| open | Anoichtá | a-neech-ta |
| closed | Kleistá | klee-sta |
| left | Aristerá | a-ree-ste-ra |
| right | Dexiá | dek-see-a |
| straight on | Eftheía | ef-thee-a |
| between | Anámesa / Metax'y | a-na-me-sa/me-tak-see |
| on the corner of… | Sti gonía tou… | stee go-nee-a too |
| near | Kontá | kon-da |
| far | Makriá | ma-kree-a |
| up | Epáno | e-pa-no |
| down | Káto | ka-to |
| early | Norís | no-rees |
| late | Argá | ar-ga |
| entrance | I eísodos | ee ee-so-thos |
| exit | I éxodos | ee e-kso-dos |
| toilet | Oi toualétes / Kateiliméni | ee-too-a-le-tes / ka-tee-lee-me-nee |
| occupied/engaged | | |
| unoccupied free/no charge | Eléftheri Doreán | e-lef-the-ree tho-re-an |
| in/out | Mésa/Exo | me-sa/ek-so |

## Making a Telephone Call

| | | |
|---|---|---|
| Where is the nearest public telephone? | Poú vrísketai o plisiéstero tilefonikós thálamos? | poo vrees-ke-teh o plee-see-e-ste-ros tee-le-fo-ni-kos tha-la-mos? |
| I would like to place a long-distance call. | Tha íthela na káno éna yperastikó tilefónima. | tha ee-the-la na ka-no e-na ee-pe-ra-sti-ko tee-le-fo-nee-ma. |
| I would like to reverse the charges. | Tha íthela na chreóso to tilefónima ston paralípti. | tha ee-the-la na chre-o-so to tee-le-fo-nee-ma ston pa-ra-lep-tee. |
| I will try again later. | Tha xanatilefoníso argótera. | tha ksa-na-tee-le-fo-ni-so ar-go-te-ra. |
| Can I leave a message? | Mporeíte na tou afísete éna mínyma? | bo-ree-te na too a-fee-se-teh e-na mee-nee-ma? |
| Could you speak up a little please? | Miláte dynatótera, parakaló? | mee-la-teh dee-na-to-te -ra, pa-ra-ka-lo? |
| Hold on. | Perímenete. | pe-ri-me-ne-teh. |
| local call | Topikó tilefónima | to-pi-ko tee-le-fo-nee-ma |
| OTE telephone office | O OTE /To tilefoneío | o O-TE /To tee-le-fo-nee-o |
| phone box/kiosk | O tilefonikós thálamos | o tee-le-fo-ni-kos tha-la-mos |
| phone card | I tilekárta | ee tee-le-kar-ta |

## Shopping

| | | |
|---|---|---|
| How much does this cost? | Póso kánei? | po-so ka-nee? |
| I would like… | Tha íthela… | tha ee-the-la… |
| Do you have…? | Echete…? | e-che-tehá? |
| I am looking for… | Apólo koitáo. | a-plos kee-ta-o. |
| Do you take credit cards/travellers' cheques? | travellers' cheques Décheste pistotikés kártes/travellers' cheques? | the-ches-teh pee-sto-tee-kes kar-tes/travellers cheques? |
| What time do you open/close? | Póte anoígete/kleínete? | po-teh a-nee-ye-teh/klee-ne-teh? |
| Can you ship this overseas? | Mporeíte na to steilete sto exoterikó? | bo-ree-teh na to stee-le-teh sto e-xo-te-ree ko? |
| This one. | Aftó edó. | af-to e-do. |
| That one. | Ekeíno. | e-kee-no. |
| expensive | Akrivó | a-kree-vo |
| cheap | Fthinó | fthee-no |
| size | To mégethos | to me-ge-thos |

| | | |
|---|---|---|
| white | **Lefkó** | *lef-ko* |
| black | **Mávro** | *mav-ro* |
| red | **Kókkino** | *ko-kee-no* |
| yellow | **Kítrino** | *kee-tree-no* |
| green | **Prásino** | *pra-see-no* |
| blue | **Mple** | *bleh* |

## Types of Shop

| | | |
|---|---|---|
| antique shop | **Magazí me antíkes** | *ma-ga-zee me an-dee-kes* |
| bakery | **O foúrnos** | *o foor-nos* |
| bank | **I trápeza** | *ee tra-pe-za* |
| bazaar | **To pazári** | *to pa-za-ree* |
| bookshop | **To vivliopoleío** | *to vee-vlee-o-po-lee-o* |
| butcher | **To kreopoleío** | *to kre-o-po-lee-o* |
| cake shop | **To zacharoplasteío** | *to za-cha-ro-pla-stee-o* |
| cheese shop | **Tirokomio** | *(tee-ro-ko-mee-o)* |
| department store | **Polykatástima** | *Po-lee-ka-ta-stee-ma* |
| fishmarket | **To ichthyopoleío/ psarádiko** | *to eech-thee-o-po-lee-o /psa-rá-dee-ko* |
| greengrocer | **To manáviko** | *to ma-na-vee-ko* |
| hairdresser | **To kommotírio** | *to ko-mo-tee-ree-o* |
| kiosk | **To períptero** | *to pe-reep-te-ro* |
| leather shop | **Magazí me dermátina eíd** | *ma-ga-zee me ther-ma-tee-na ee-thee* |
| street market | **I laïkí agorá** | *ee la-ee-kee a-go-ra* |
| newsagent | **O efimeridopólis** | *O e-fee-me-ree-tho-po-lees* |
| pharmacy | **To farmakeío** | *to far-ma-kee-o* |
| post office | **To tachydromeío** | *to ta-chee-thro-mee-o* |
| shoe shop | **Katástima me podimáton** | *ka-ta-stee-ma me po-dee-ma-ton* |
| souvenir shop | **Magazí me "souvenir"** | *meh "souvenir"* |
| supermarket | **"Supermarket" / Yperagorá** | *"Supermarket" / ee-per-a-go-ra* |
| tobacconist | **Eídi kapnistoú** | *Ee-thee kap-nees-* |
| travel agent | **To taxeidiotikó grafeío** | *to tak-see-thy-o-tee-ko gra-fee-o* |

## Sightseeing

| | | |
|---|---|---|
| tourist information | **O EOT** | *o E-OT* |
| tourist police | **I touristikí astynomía** | *ee too-rees-tee-kee a-stee-no-mee-a* |
| archaeological | **archaiologikós** | *ar-che-o-lo-gee-kos* |
| art gallery | **I gkalerí** | *ee ga-le-ree* |
| beach | **I paralía** | *ee pa-ra-lee-a* |
| Byzantine | **vyzantinós** | *vee-zan-dee-nos* |
| castle | **To kástro** | *to ka-stro* |
| cathedral | **I mitrópoli** | *ee mee-tro-po-lee* |
| cave | **To spílaio** | *to spee-le-o* |
| church | **I ekklisía** | *ee e-klee-see-a* |
| folk art | **laïkí téchni** | *la-ee-kee tech-nee* |
| fountain | **To syntriváni** | *to seen-dree-va-nee* |
| garden | **O kípos** | *o kee-pos* |
| gorge | **To farángi** | *to fa-ran-gee* |
| grave of…. | **O táfos tou…** | *o ta-fos too* |
| hill | **O lófos** | *o lo-fos* |
| historical | **istorikós** | *ee-sto-ree-kos* |
| island | **To nisí** | *to nee-see* |
| lake | **I límni** | *ee leem-nee* |
| library | **I vivliothíki** | *ee veev-lee-o-thee-kee* |
| mansion | **I épavlis** | *ee e-pav-lees* |
| monastery | **moní** | *mo-ni* |
| mountain | **To vounó** | *to voo-no* |
| municipal | **dimotikós** | *thee-mo-tee-kos* |
| museum | **To mouseío** | *to moo-se-o* |
| national | **ethnikós** | *eth-nee-kos* |
| park | **To párko** | *to par-ko* |
| river | **To potámi** | *to po-ta-mee* |
| road | **O drómos** | *o thro-mos* |
| saint | **ágios/ágioi/ agía/agíes** | *a-yee-os/a-yee-ee/a-yee-a/ a-yee-es* |
| spring | **I pigí** | *ee pee-yee* |
| square | **I plateía** | *ee pla-tee-a* |
| stadium | **To stádio** | *to sta-thee-o* |
| statue | **To ágalma** | *to a-gal-ma* |
| theatre | **To théatro** | *to the-a-tro* |
| town hall | **To dimarcheío** | *to thee-mar-chee-o* |
| closed on public holidays | **kleistó tis argíes** | *klee-sto tees aryee-es* |

## Transport

| | | |
|---|---|---|
| When does the … leave? | **Póte févgei to…?** | *po-teh fev-yee to…?* |
| Where is the bus stop? | **Poú eínai i stási tou leoforeíou?** | *poo ee-neh ee sta-see too le-o-fo-ree-oo…?* |
| Is there a bus to? | **Ypárchei leoforeío gia…?** | *ee-par-chee le-o-fo-ree-o yia…?* |
| ticket office | **Ekdotíria eisitiríon** | *Ek-tho-tee-reea ee-see-tee-ree-on* |
| return ticket | **Eisitírio me epistrofí** | *ee-see-tee-ree-o meh e-pee-stro-fee* |
| single journey | **Apló eisitírio** | *a-plo ee-see-tee-reeo* |
| bus station | **O stathmós leoforeíon** | *o stath-mos leo-fo-ree-on* |
| bus ticket | **Eisitírio leoforeíou** | *ee-see-tee-ree-o leo-fo-ree-oo* |
| trolley bus | **To trólley** | *to tro-le-ee* |
| port | **To limáni** | *to lee-ma-nee* |
| train/metro | **To tréno** | *to tre-no* |
| railway station | **sidirodromikós stathmós** | *see-thee-ro-thro-mee-kos stath-mos* |
| moped | **To motopodílato/ To michanáki** | *to mo-to-po-thee-la-to/to mee-cha-na-kee* |
| bicycle | **To podílato** | *to po-thee-la-to* |
| taxi | **To taxí** | *to tak-see* |
| airport | **To aerodrómio** | *to a-e-ro-thro-mee-o* |
| ferry | **To "ferry-boat"** | *to fe-ree-bot* |
| hydrofoil | **To delfíni / To ydroptérygo** | *to del-fee-nee /To ee-throp-te-ree-go* |
| catamaran for hire | **To katamarán Enoikiázontai** | *to catamaran e-nee-kya-zon-deh* |

## Staying in a Hotel

| | | |
|---|---|---|
| Do you have a vacant room? | **Echete domátia?** | *e-che-teh tho-ma-tee-a?* |
| I have a reservation. | **Echo kánei krátisi.** | *e-cho ka-nee kra-tee-see.* |
| double room with double bed | **Díklino me dipló kreváti** | *thee-klee-no meh thee-plo kre-va-tee* |
| twin room | **Díklino me dipló kreváti** | *thee-klee-no meh mo-na kre-vat-ya* |
| single room | **Monóklino** | *mo-no-klee-no* |
| room with a bath | **Domátio me mpánio** | *tho-ma-tee-o meh ban-yo* |
| shower | **To douz** | *To douz* |
| porter | **O portiéris** | *o por-tye-rees* |
| key | **To kleidí** | *to klee-dee* |
| room with a sea view/balcony | **Domátio me théa sti thálassa/ mpalkóni** | *tho-ma-tee-o meh the-a stee tha-la-sa/bal-ko-nee* |
| Does the price include breakfast? | **To proïnó symperilamvánetai stin timí?** | *to pro-ee-no seem-be-ree-lam-va-ne-teh steen tee-mee?* |

## Eating Out

| | | |
|---|---|---|
| Have you got a table? | **Echete trapézi?** | *e-che-te tra-pe-zee?* |

| English | Greek | Pronunciation |
|---|---|---|
| I want to reserve a table. | Thélo na kratíso éna trapézi. | the-lo na kra-tee-so e-na tra-pe-zee. |
| The bill, please. | Ton logariazmó, parakaló | ton lo-gar-yas-mo pa-ra-ka-lo parakaló. |
| I am a vegetarian. | Eímai chortofágos. | ee-meh chor-to-fa-gos. |
| What is fresh today? | Ti frésko échete símera? | tee fres-ko e-che-teh see-me-ra? |
| waiter/waitress | K'yrie/Garson"/ Kyría | Kee-ree-eh/Gar-son/Kee-ree-a |
| menu | O katálogos | o ka-ta-lo-gos |
| cover charge | To "couvert" | to koo-ver |
| wine list | O katálogos me ta oinopnevmatódi | o ka-ta-lo-gos meh ta ee-no-pnev-ma-to-thee |
| glass | To potíri | to po-tee-ree |
| bottle | To mpoukáli | to bou-ka-lee |
| knife | To machaíri | to ma-che-ree |
| fork | To pirouni | to pee-roo-nee |
| spoon | To koutáli | to koo-ta-lee |
| breakfast | To proïnó | to pro-ee-no |
| lunch | To mesimerianó | to me-see-mer-ya-no |
| dinner | To deípno | to theep-no |
| main course | To kyrios gévma | to kee-ree-os yev-ma |
| starter/first course | Ta orektiká | ta-o-rek-tee-ka |
| dessert | To glykó | to ylee-ko |
| dish of the day | To piáto tis i méras | to pya-to tees ee-me-ras |
| bar | To "bar" | To bar |
| taverna | I tavérna | ee ta-ver-na |
| café | To kafeneío | to ka-fe-nee-o |
| fish taverna | I psarotavérna | ee psa-ro-ta-ver-na |
| grill house | I psistariá | ee psee-sta-rya |
| wine shop | To oinopoleío | to ee-no-po-lee-o |
| dairy shop | To galaktopoleío | to ga-lak-to-po-lee-o |
| restaurant | To estiatório | toe-stee-a-to-ree-o |
| ouzeri | To ouzerí | to oo-ze-ree |
| meze shop | To mezedopoleío | To me-ze-do-po-lee-o |
| take away kebabs | To souvlatzídiko | To soo-vlat-zee-dee-ko |
| rare | Eláchista psiméno | e-lach-ees-ta psee-me-no |
| medium | Métria psiméno | met-ree-a psee-me-no |
| well done | Kalopsiméno | ka-lo-psee-me-no |

**Basic Food and Drink**

| English | Greek | Pronunciation |
|---|---|---|
| coffee | kafés | o ka-fes |
| with milk | me gála | me ga-la |
| black coffee | skétos | ske-tos cho-rees |
| without sugar | chorís záchari | za-cha-ree |
| medium sweet | métrios | me-tree-os |
| very sweet | glykó | glee-kees |
| tea | tsái | tsa-ee |
| hot chocolate | zestí sokoláta | ze-stee so-ko-la-ta |
| wine | krasí | kra-see |
| red | kókkino | ko-kee-no |
| white | lefkó | lef-ko |
| rosé | rozé | ro-ze |
| raki | To rakí | to ra-kee |
| ouzo | To oúzo | to oo-zo |
| retsina | I retsína | ee ret-see-na |
| water | To neró | to ne-ro |
| octopus | To chtapódi | to chta-po-dee |
| fish | To psári | to psa-ree |
| cheese | To tyrí | to tee-ree |
| halloumi | To chaloúmi | to cha-loo-mee |
| feta | I féta | ee fe-ta |
| bread | To psomí | to pso-mee |
| bean soup | I fasoláda | ee fa-so-la-tha |
| houmous | To houmous | to choo-moos |
| halva | O chalvás | o chal-vas |
| meat kebabs | O g'yros | o yee-ros |

| English | Greek | Pronunciation |
|---|---|---|
| Turkish delight | To loukoúmi | to loo-koo-mee |
| baklava | O mpaklavás | o bak-la-vas |
| klephtiko | To kléftiko | to klef-tee-ko |

**Numbers**

| English | Greek | Pronunciation |
|---|---|---|
| 1 | éna | e-na |
| 2 | d'yo | thee-o |
| 3 | tría | tree-a |
| 4 | téssera | te-se-ra |
| 5 | pénte | pen-deh |
| 6 | éxi | ek-si |
| 7 | eptá | ep-ta |
| 8 | ochtó | och-to |
| 9 | ennéa | e-ne-a |
| 10 | déka | the-ka |
| 11 | énteka | en-de-ka |
| 12 | dódeka | tho-the-ka |
| 13 | dekatría | de-ka-tree-a |
| 14 | dekatéssera | the-ka-tes-se-ra |
| 15 | dekapénte | the-ka-pen-de |
| 16 | dekaéxi | the-ka-ek-si |
| 17 | dekaeptá | the-ka-ep-ta |
| 18 | dekaochtó | the-ka-och-to |
| 19 | dekaennéa | the-ka-e-ne-a |
| 20 | eíkosi | ee-ko-see |
| 21 | eikosiéna | ee-ko-see-e-na |
| 30 | triánta | tree-an-da |
| 40 | saránta | sa-ran-da |
| 50 | penínta | pe-neen-da |
| 60 | exínta | ek-seen-da |
| 70 | evdomínta | ev-tho-meen-da |
| 80 | ogdónta | og-thon-da |
| 90 | enenínta | e-ne-neen-da |
| 100 | ekató | e-ka-to |
| 200 | diakósia | thya-kos-ya |
| 1,000 | chília | cheel-ya |
| 2,000 | d'yo chiliádes | thee-o cheel-ya-thes |
| 1,000,000 | éna ekatommýrio | e-na e-ka-to-mee-ree-o |
| one minute | éna leptó | e-na lep-to |
| one hour | mía óra | mee-a o-ra |
| half an hour | misí óra | mee-see o-ra |
| quarter of an hour | éna tétarto | e-na te-tar-to |
| half past one | mía kai misí | mee-a keh mee-see |
| quarter past one | mía kai tétarto | mee-a keh te-tar-to |
| ten past one | mía kai déka | mee-a keh the-ka |
| quarter to two | d'yo pará tétarto | thee-o pa-ra te-tar-to |
| ten to two | d'yo pará déka | thee-o pa-ra the-ka |
| a day | mía méra | mee-a me-ra |
| a week | mía evdomáda | mee-a ev-tho-ma-tha |
| a month | énas mínas | e-nas mee-nas |
| a year | énas chrónos | e-nas chro-nos |
| Monday | Deftéra | thef-te-ra |
| Tuesday | Tríti | tree-tee |
| Wednesday | Tetárti | te-tar-tee |
| Thursday | Pémpti | pemp-tee |
| Friday | Paraskeví | pa-ras-ke-vee |
| Saturday | Sávvato | sa-va-to |
| Sunday | Kyriakí | keer-ee-a-kee |
| January | Ianouários | ee-a-noo-a-ree-os |
| February | Fevrouários | fev-roo-a-ree-os |
| March | Mártios | mar-tee-os |
| April | Aprílios | a-pree-lee-os |
| May | Máios | ma-ee-os |
| June | Ioúnios | ee-oo-nee-os |
| July | Ioúlios | ee-oo-lee-os |
| August | Avgoustos | av-goo-stos |
| September | Septémvrios | sep-tem-vree-os |
| October | Októvrios | ok-to-vree-os |
| November | Noémvrios | no-em-vree-os |
| December | Dekémvrios | the-kem-vree-os |